THEY MADE IT
IN AMERICA

THEY MADE IT IN AMERICA

A Celebration of the Achievements of Great Italian Americans

ROBERT CORTE

WILLIAM MORROW AND COMPANY, INC.
New York

Library of Congress Cataloging-in-Publication Data

Corte, Robert.
    They made it in America : a celebration of the achievements of
great Italian Americans / by Robert Corte.
        p.   cm.
    Includes bibliographical references.
    ISBN 0-688-10778-8
    1. Italian-American   artists—Biography.   2. Italian-American
arts.
    I. Title.
NX512.3.I85C67   1993
700'.92'273—dc20
    [B]   92-27160
                                                                    CIP

Printed in the United States of America

First Edition

1 2 3 4 5 6 7 8 9 10

BOOK DESIGN BY PAUL CHEVANNES

Contents

Joltin' Joe DiMaggio, also known as "The Yankee Clipper," watching one of his 361 career home runs sail out over the outfield fence AMERICAN STOCK PHOTOS

A Gentleman at Bat

•◣◥•◣◥•◣◥•◣◥•◣◥•◣◥•◣◥•◣◥•◣◥•

THE NEW YORK YANKEES were not a happy team following the game they played against the Chicago White Sox on May 15, 1941. They had been thrashed by a score of thirteen to one. But that dismal game had also seen the beginning of what was to become one of the most legendary feats in the history of the team and indeed of baseball itself. Center fielder Joe DiMaggio had gotten a hit that day, a clean single, and he would go on getting a hit in every game for the next two months.

There was a war going on in Europe, one that many Americans feared their country would eventually become involved in, but as "the streak" continued, millions turned to the sports pages first to see how "Joltin' Joe" was doing.

June 10, 1941: Joe breaks his own major-league record of hits in twenty-three consecutive games.

June 14: Joe surpasses the record of earlier Yankee immortal Babe Ruth.

June 21: The National League record of thirty-three games compiled by Hall of Famer Rogers Hornsby is broken.

June 29: The all-time record of Wee Willie Keeler, a forty-four-game streak recorded in 1897, is knocked out of the realm of legend.

July 17: At Cleveland's Municipal Stadium, 67,468 baseball fans, the largest crowd up to that time for a night game, turns out to watch the Indians play the Yankees. Joe DiMaggio had now hit safely in an incredible fifty-six games in a row. In his first at-bat, Joe hits a slasher past third base. Playing deep, American League All-Star third baseman Ken Keltner makes an "impossible" backhanded catch.

His second time up, DiMaggio is walked. The third time up, he hits another hard one down the third-base line. Ken Keltner repeats his heroics. ("All I was trying to do," Keltner would later tell DiMaggio, "was to prevent a two-base hit.")

Joltin' Joe gets one more chance in the eighth inning, but it is caught by future Hall of Fame shortstop Lou Boudreau, ending the streak. After that one break, though, DiMaggio would go on to hit safely in the next sixteen games.

Q. DiMaggio had also had a remarkable streak while playing for the San Francisco Seals in the minor leagues. Had that streak come close to his legendary major-league record of 1941?

A. Yes, it surpassed it. Not yet nineteen, DiMaggio hit safely in sixty-one straight games.

Because of the much greater use of relief pitchers in contemporary baseball, most experts on the sport believe that Joe DiMaggio's fifty-six-game streak is a record that cannot be broken. But there was a great deal more to "The Yankee Clipper," as he came to be called, than this signal achievement.

Born November 25, 1914, in Martinez, California, the eighth of nine children (older brother Vince and the baby of the family, Dom, were also major-league players), this son of

a fisherman came to be regarded as one of the greatest "gentle-
men" ever to play the game. There were innumerable personal
achievements, including batting titles in 1939 and 1940 (.361
and .352—he lost by one percentage point to Ted Williams's
.406 in 1941), and the Most Valuable Player Award in 1941
and 1947, the latter after three years' service in World War
II. But he was unselfish to the point that the great Connie
Mack called him "the greatest team player that ever lived."

A reporter once asked Joe DiMaggio why he always seemed
to give 100 percent, no matter what. His answer was: "There
is always some kid who may be seeing me for the first time or
the last time. I owe him my best." That comes close to saying
it all.

A Cavalryman First

●~●~●~●~●~●~●~●~●~●~●~●~●~●~●~●~●

FEW ITALIAN AMERICANS HAVE had more colorful lives than
Luigi Palma di Cesnola—or, to give him his full due,
Count Emmanuele Pietro Paolo Maria Luigi Palma di Cesnola. He was a man of bold and diverse talents who seemed
always to act as a lightning rod for controversy, but he had an
astonishing ability to ride on through the turmoil that so often
surrounded him to achieve what he had set out to do.

Cesnola was a cavalryman who became the youngest officer
in King Charles Albert's Royal Army of the Piedmont at the
age of sixteen, commissioned on the field at the Battle of
Novara in 1849. But his first military career was derailed by
a scandal, rumored to involve a woman, and by 1860, he was
en route from Constantinople to New York by ship.

He had a very difficult time and had to support himself by
giving French and Italian lessons. One of his students was a
thirty-year-old member of New York society named Mary
Reid, who had recently inherited a considerable estate. She
fell in love with her teacher, and despite the pleas of friends
and relatives, they were married in June 1861. It proved to be
a marriage of remarkable stability in an otherwise tumultuous
life.

The outbreak of the Civil War gave Cesnola a chance to

apply his skills as a cavalryman. Commissioned as a lieutenant colonel, Cesnola was an extremely brave and capable officer, with one serious problem: He was constantly at odds with his senior officers, most of whom, in fact, did not have the experience Cesnola had. Twice he was arrested on the orders of outraged commanders whose tactics he had disparaged or disobeyed. The first time, he was granted a new commission because of the protests of the men he commanded. The second time, one of his men rode back to where he was being held and begged him to enter the fierce battle at Aldie Gap in Virginia. There, he was captured and imprisoned at Richmond's infamous Libby Prison for several days, but his bravery at Aldie Gap would eventually earn him the Congressional Medal of Honor—nearly thirty-four years later, in 1897.

Cesnola fought again with distinction with Sheridan's forces, but was mustered out in September 1864, because his unit had completed its term of enlistment. Seeking both an advancement in rank and a government position, Cesnola met with Lincoln two days before the president was assassinated. Cesnola said that Lincoln had agreed to make him a brigadier general, but there was no reference to this among Lincoln's papers. Cesnola nevertheless called himself general for the rest of his life, and swore under oath several times that that had been Lincoln's intention.

As a result of his meeting with Lincoln, however, Cesnola was appointed consul to Cyprus—a position that would bring him not one, but two, new careers. Although both Cesnola and his wife were much dismayed by their first impression of Cyprus, they settled in to make the best of his posting to this large primitive island administered by Turkey. Because of its strategic importance, Cyprus was host to a good-size diplomatic community, many of whose members amused themselves with amateurish archeological digs. Cesnola became fascinated by this pursuit—even obsessed—and soon was so involved that other diplomats left the field—in all senses of the word—to him. He began unearthing prodigious amounts of buried statuary, pottery, and other artifacts, including gold necklaces and chalices. A temple site at Golgos was particularly rich in large statues.

Because of regular flare-ups between the Turks and Greeks, Cesnola did have to attend to diplomatic duties at times, especially since by the late 1860s he was also representing Greece and Russia, a fact that complicated his diplomatic chores but would prove invaluable in ultimately getting his treasures off Cyprus and back to America. Having spent a great deal of his and his wife's money to carry out his digs, he found it necessary to recoup. There was interest from a Paris antiquities dealer, from the Hermitage Museum in St. Petersburg, and from the British Museum. But the Franco-Prussian War disrupted negotiations, and he was finally left with one last hope—the fledgling Metropolitan Museum of Art in New York City, whose building was only barely under construction.

Before he could consider their offer, though, he had to get his collection off Cyprus, because the Turkish government was on the verge of seizing it. He was given a direct order that prohibited him in his capacity as the American consul to ship the goods. The versatile diplomat therefore shipped them as the property of the Russian consul—the authorities in Constantinople having overlooked the fact that he was doing double, even triple, duty.

Cesnola arranged for an article to be published in the July 1871 issue of the prestigious *Harper's New Monthly Magazine* outlining his finds, and as he had hoped, the trustees of the Metropolitan Museum took the bait. He was offered fifty thousand dollars for his treasures, and arrangements were made for him to be paid for his cataloging them. The exhibition opened in March 1873 in a New York City mansion that served as the new museum's temporary display space. The exhibition was a great success.

Leaving his wife and children in America, Cesnola returned to Cyprus. There, at a site that others had surveyed without success, he came upon what would become known as the Treasure of Curium. While the earlier digs had been thin in terms of gold objects, Curium was packed with them.

The Metropolitan came through again. Not only did the trustees agree to purchase the new treasure, they also offered him the post of first director of the museum. When the new building finally opened on the Upper East Side of New York City in March 1880, its proud director, Luigi Palma di Cesnola, had the privilege of showing President Rutherford B. Hayes, present for the ceremonies, around his domain.

Cesnola continued as director of the Metropolitan until his death in 1904. There were controversies along the way—with Cesnola there were always controversies—but by the time of his death, he had been director of the museum for twenty-five years, laid the foundations of its world-renowned collection in many areas, including the acquisition of paintings by Vermeer, Manet, Van Dyck, Winslow Homer, and Delacroix.

Perhaps most important to the proud old cavalryman was his Congressional Medal of Honor. There was no one who would even think of addressing him as anything other than General Cesnola. His funeral at St. Patrick's Cathedral was attended not just by the leaders of the Italian community, but by the titans of Wall Street and the most important names in New York society. General Luigi Palma di Cesnola had more than made his mark on his adopted country.

The Greater Victory

●◄●◄●◄●◄●◄●◄●◄●◄●◄●◄●◄●◄●

IN 1948, ANDY VARIPAPA did something no one else had ever before accomplished. For the second year in a row, he had won bowling's All-Star Individual Match Game championship. News reports of his victory almost always made mention of the nickname he had recently acquired: "Bowling's Talking Machine." Andy Varipapa was probably prouder of that nickname than he was of his bowling ability. It had been earned the hard way.

Varipapa had been regarded as one of the world's best bowlers since 1930, when, at the age of thirty-six, he had burst onto the scene out of the far reaches of Brooklyn, where he worked as a toolmaker. Living in the United States since 1903, when his family had emigrated from Calabria, Italy (he was nine years old and knew no English), he was now becoming famous. But he still had problems with his English, as well as speaking with a heavy Brooklynese accent that was almost incomprehensible to anyone outside of New York City. He began getting offers to appear at bowling exhibitions around the country, but that meant lecturing on the fine points of the game, and he knew that he wouldn't be understood.

So Varipapa began working just as hard on his English as he did on his bowling. Four years later, he was ready to branch out. He made a tour of Midwest towns around major cities. His English had improved a lot but was far from flawless, so in each town, Andy not only bowled but also went to the movies, listening carefully then practicing his diction as he drove on to the next town. He learned a lot of bowling tricks in the small towns of mid-America over the next ten years, so many that he was able to astonish people with his shots when he was well into his sixties. He had also learned English so well that he was given his new nickname: "Bowling's Talking Machine." This, Andy Varipapa regarded as the best trophy of them all.

Banker to the
Common Man

▰▰▰▰▰▰▰▰▰▰▰▰▰▰▰▰▰▰▰▰▰▰▰▰

BEFORE DAWN ON APRIL 18, 1906, San Francisco, California, was rocked by what came to be known as the Great Earthquake. The shifting of the earth caused considerable destruction in some areas, but the terrible fires that continued for nearly a week caused much greater damage. At his home, Seven Oaks, twenty-five miles away in San Mateo, Amadeo Giannini was wakened by the tremors and immediately set off for San Francisco, where he had opened a small bank in a converted saloon on October 17, 1904.

Several of his employees who lived in the city were already at the bank. Concerned about the possibility of fire, Giannini enlisted the help of his employees in loading the bank's cash reserves, about eighty thousand dollars in gold, into sacks and orange crates; these in turn were loaded onto a horse-drawn wagon that looked like any of hundreds of produce wagons to be seen in the area. He also loaded onto the wagon something that proved especially important to his fledgling bank over the next few weeks: his records of customer deposits. The wagon was covered with fruit and vegetables, and with two assistants dressed as vendors, he made his way out of the city. On the outskirts, he stopped at the house of a friend and substituted bedding and furniture for the produce. The roads out of San Francisco had many such wagons traversing them that day as families fled the burning city. There were no problems in reaching Seven Oaks late that night.

Almost all the other banks in San Francisco lost their records in the uncontrollable fires, and a bank holiday was declared that lasted nearly a month. Giannini, however, was able to reopen in five days, with a "branch" at the home of younger brother Attilo, a doctor, and most famously on Washington Wharf, where he operated from a plank balanced between two barrels. Giannini was already beloved and deeply trusted by his fellow Italian Americans, many of whom had bought hundred-dollar shares in the bank before it opened. Now he became a San Francisco legend. On the wharf he began making loans with the eighty thousand dollars in gold that represented one tenth of the bank's deposits, asking people to accept half of what they asked for, so that he could help as many people as possible.

Q. Why did Giannini ask men who wanted loans but who were not known to him personally (and he knew most of his depositors by sight and even name) to show him their hands?

A. He wanted to see if they were calloused from work. If they were, that was collateral enough for him.

Amadeo knew what calloused hands meant. He had had them himself as a young man. His parents had come to America from the Ligurian area of Italy in 1869; Luigi was twenty-two, his wife, Virginia, just fifteen. Arriving in California on the recently completed transcontinental railroad, they settled first in San Jose, where Luigi leased a twenty-room boarding-house. Amadeo Peter Giannini was born there on May 6, 1870. His parents saved enough money to buy a forty-acre farm south of San Francisco, and two more boys were born. When Amadeo was only seven, his father was stabbed to death by a neighbor in a fight over a single dollar. His mother and a friend of the family, Lorenzo Scatena, were married two years later. Scatena got along well with all three boys, but there was a particular bond between him and Amadeo. Scatena started a wholesale produce business in San Francisco when Amadeo was twelve, and the six-foot-tall youngster was working for his stepfather full time at the age of fifteen. Amadeo was a hard worker and popular with everyone, and his stepfather made him a full partner when he was twenty-one.

The company was successful enough and Amadeo more than handsome enough to successfully court the daughter of a wealthy real estate owner, Joseph Cuneo. Amadeo and Clorinda were married in 1892, both twenty-two years old, and soon moved to Seven Oaks, where they would live out their lives despite the vast successes that Amadeo would achieve. Giannini went into real estate himself, and when his father-in-law died in 1902, the Cuneo family—there were eleven children—asked Giannini to take charge of their father's holdings in return for 25 percent of all profits. More important, this new responsibility brought with it Joseph Cuneo's place as a director of a modest bank, the Columbus Savings and Loan Society, most of whose depositors were immigrant Italian Americans.

Columbus Savings was a very conservative institution and Giannini chafed at its refusal to do more for the poorer people among the immigrant population, which was continually growing. That led him to seek the money, largely in one-hundred-dollar shares, to open his own bank. Called the Bank of Italy, it opened for business on October 17, 1904. Under the guidance of Giannini, it would eventually become the Bank of America, with the largest holdings of any bank in the world.

When the Bank of Italy reopened in a former real estate office following the San Francisco fire, word of Giannini's optimistic and forward-looking stand on Washington Wharf had taken on the aura of a North Beach legend, and immigrants who had never entrusted their money to a bank before doubled his number of depositors by the end of the year. The following year, forseeing that the bank panic that was moving around the world would eventually hit San Francisco, Giannini took the steps of cutting back on loans in order to build up reserves, as well as persuading customers to deal more often in paper money; so when the crisis came, he had gold piled high where it could be seen behind bars. There was no run on the Bank of Italy.

Giannini was convinced that the future of banking lay with branch offices—an idea that was regarded with great suspicion in the established banking community. There was considerable derision for this man who, in fact, understood that the economic future of America lay with its most ordinary citizens. His own people had great faith in him, but this in itself was cause for disdain in many circles. One of the consequences was that Giannini began signing himself A.P. instead of Amadeo Peter. The initials sat much better with the often anti-Italian establishment figures he found himself dealing with more and more often. But he continued to answer his own phone at his bank, and his ability to make his depositors feel that he cared about them personally never faltered.

> **Q.** By 1919, the Bank of Italy had the fourth-largest holdings of any bank in California. It also had nearly one hundred ninety thousand depositors. How did that compare to other banks in California and around the country?
>
> **A.** No other bank across the nation, even in New York City, had as many.

Giannini's Bank of Italy continued to grow at an astonishing pace, opening branches and acquiring other banks. Antitrust laws stood in the way of his creating a truly national, and ultimately international, bank, but he went about setting up the building blocks for such an entity within the restrictions of the law.

Giannini's first acquisition in another state—facilitated by setting up a new holding company—was the East River National Bank of New York. Leaders of the New York City Italian-American community had been after him for years to take such a step. This move in 1919 was followed by the purchase, in 1925, of New York's Bowery National Bank, which he then merged with the East River. His boldest step, in 1928, was to buy the Bank of America on Wall Street, a bank with great prestige, although modest holdings. This acquisition inevitably raised the ire of the establishment Wall Street bankers, who decided the onetime fruit vendor was getting far too uppity. In retaliation, Wall Street played a behind-the-scenes role in fomenting a panic by driving up the price of Bank of Italy shares and then suddenly dumping them.

Giannini went to Rome for a rest and to do business connected with his Italian bank, Banca Italia Meridonale, which had been created during the 1920s out of a number of small Italian institutions. Although he was ill, Giannini marshalled himself, and with his son Mario, who had become his right-hand man, purchased sixty million dollars in shares to stop the panic, at an estimated eventual loss of twenty million dollars.

Further problems awaited him. In his ongoing pursuit of a national bank, Giannini had created a huge holding company called Transamerica, headed by a New York financier named Elisha Walker. The San Francisco–based Bank of Italy was given the new name Bank of America in 1930. Transamerica was, for legal reasons, the parent company of Bank of America. When Transamerica's stock began to fall, Walker announced that he would sell Bank of America. There had already been difficulties between the two men—in the aftermath of the 1929 crash Giannini urged continued expansion and Walker retrenchment—now the split in philosophy turned into a titanic struggle for control.

Giannini was again in Italy. Seriously ill with polyneuritis, he astonished his doctors by making an unexpected recovery. He returned to America and began an effort to capture enough proxy votes to regain control. Financial experts and journalists scoffed. But the "little people," the Italian-American workers and small businessmen who had bought his stock because he believed in them, once again showed that they also believed in him. When the showdown came, Giannini had 67 percent of the proxy votes and was yet again in full control of the bank he had founded.

Through the rest of the 1930s and the war years the Bank of America continued to grow and prosper. By 1946 it had become the largest privately held bank in the world. Its founder was officially retired but still had a major say in plans for the bank's future.

When the onetime fruit vendor died at Seven Oaks of a heart attack shortly after his seventy-ninth birthday, obituaries paid homage to a man of genius. His personal estate was less than a half-million dollars (he had never been interested in the vast mansions and yachts so beloved of most titans of finance and had always kept his own remuneration modest), and the estate was largely given over to a charitable foundation he had established four years earlier to finance the educations of the bank's employees. He had never gone to college. He was the kind of genius for whom it wasn't necessary, but he fully understood its importance to those in the new world he had helped create.

Mother to the Poor

●•●•●•●•●•●•●•●•●•●•●•●•●•●•●•●•●

NEAR SANT'ANGELO LODIGIANO, in Italy's Lombardy region, Maria Francesca Cabrini, the youngest of thirteen children, was born on July 15, 1850. After the deaths of her parents she tried twice to become a nun, but was refused twice because of her health. Undaunted, and with a strong belief that she had a calling to help the poor, she persuaded Cardinal Parocchi to give her an orphanage to run at Cadogno. This ultimately became the mother house of the Missionary Sisters of the Sacred Heart, of which she was the founder.

Her efforts caught the attention of Pope Leo XIII, who was noted for his concern for the poor, and after her first audience with him, he became her champion. Archbishop Corrigan of New York City had been seeking the help of the Vatican in finding someone to work with the poor Italian immigrants who had settled in large numbers in New York, and Pope Leo chose Maria Francesca Cabrini. Known in America as Mother Cabrini, she arrived in the United States with six nuns in 1889.

In New York she found large numbers of Italians working sixteen-hour days at subsistence wages and living in squalor, with many orphaned or abandoned children roaming the streets. Mother Cabrini put her remarkable faith, tenacity, and charm to work. Beginning with an orphanage on East Fifty-ninth Street, she established an astonishing network of schools, orphanages, hospitals, and convents, the majority in the United States (of which she became a citizen in 1909) but also in Central and South America, Italy, France, and England. Constantly traveling, persuading bishops, cardinals and private donors to provide buildings, and drawing on the burgeoning Italian communities themselves for donations of all kinds, she succeeded in opening a total of sixty-seven educational and medical facilities over the course of the next twenty-seven years: among them, Columbus Hospital (now known as Cabrini Medical Center) in New York, two hospitals in Chicago, another in Wyoming, a school in southern California, a sanatorium in Washington—she traveled wherever there was need, and never failed to bring her plans to fruition.

Overseeing the opening of a hospital and mission in Brazil in 1908, she came down with malaria, which undermined her health but could not stop her from carrying out new projects for another nine years. She died of a heart attack on December 22, 1917, but by then she had missions all over the Western World carrying on her vision. Supplication to Mother Cabrini by the ill, became widespread and led to numerous extraordinary cures that fostered an early call for her elevation to sainthood. She was ultimately canonized in 1946, becoming the first American to be named a Roman Catholic saint. The body of Saint Frances Xavier Cabrini is enshrined in New York City, and her feast day is November 13.

The Man from Nicetown

●━●━●━●━●━●━●━●━●━●━●━●━●━●━●━●━●

FITTINGLY, THE MAN WHO would become the most beloved of all the scrappy Brooklyn Dodgers was born in a section of North Philadelphia known as Nicetown. In discussing the belated acceptance into major-league baseball of black players, the great sportswriter Red Smith saluted the breaking of the color line by the legendary Jackie Robinson, but went on to say, "Roy Campanella is the one who made friends."

This son of an immigrant father from Sicily and an African-American mother, born November 19, 1921, was as joyful a man as ever played the game of baseball. He was first hired as a catcher when he was only fifteen, and he loved the game so much that even twelve long years as a "gypsy" player all across the United States and in South America did nothing to sour his sunny disposition. Often in those years he played as many as three hundred games, throughout the calendar, for no more than three hundred dollars a month. As a result, by the time he joined the Brooklyn Dodgers in 1948, he was as experienced and as savvy as any man who ever crouched behind a plate.

He was a genius at calling for the right pitch at the right moment, but he was also a great hitter and a sterling defensive player who threw out two of every three base runners who tried to steal on him. "Campy," as everyone called him, could do it all. He was the National League's Most Valuable Player in 1951, 1953, and 1955, and helped lead the Dodgers to five World Series. His half-Italian heritage made him the perfect ballplayer for the fans in Brooklyn, with its large Italian-American population. When it was announced that the Dodgers would move to Los Angeles for the 1958 season, it wasn't just the loss of their team that enraged the Brooklyn fans; but also the loss of Campanella.

As it turned out, the new fans in Los Angeles wouldn't have that privilege, either. On January 28, 1958, Roy Campanella's car skidded on an icy patch of highway, and he was left paralyzed for life. In 1959, when he had recovered sufficiently to make the trip, Roy flew to California for a special tribute to him during an exhibition game between the Los Angeles Dodgers and the New York Yankees. The Los Angeles Coliseum was jammed by 93,103 fans—the largest crowd ever to attend a baseball game, but it was Roy, not the game itself, they were there for. The lights in the stadium were dimmed and all was dark for a moment. Then everyone in the vast assemblage lit a match and held it aloft in tribute.

The fans never did forget Roy. And neither did the sportswriters. In 1969, his last year of eligibility, the writers voted Roy Campanella into the Hall of Fame, even though he had played fewer than ten years in the major league.

Music by Mancini

●▬●▬●▬●▬●▬●▬●▬●▬●▬●▬●▬●▬●▬●

WITH SEVENTEEN OSCAR NOMINATIONS and an even greater number of Grammy nominations over the course of the past four decades, Enrico Nicola Mancini, known as Henry, has been one of the most dominant and versatile composers of songs, scores, and theme music for movies and television since the advent of recorded sound. Equally at home composing for a dark thriller like Orson Welles's *Touch of Evil* (1958), a farce like *The Pink Panther* (1964), or a biographical melodrama like *Mommie Dearest* (1981), he can draw on a wide variety of musical modes, from jazz to big band to Latin rhythm to a swelling-strings romanticism.

Mancini was born in Cleveland, Ohio, on April 16, 1924, but the family soon moved to Pennsylvania. There his father, a steelworker and music lover who played the flute in the local Sons of Italy band, saw to it that young Enrico learned to play several musical instruments, including picolo, flute, and piano. He got a first-rate musical education at the Carnegie Institute in Philadelphia and the Juilliard School of Music in New York. Following army infantry service in World War II, he became a member of the reorganized Glenn Miller Band— he'd known the Miller arrangements since he was in high school. Hired by Universal-International in 1952, he received his first Academy Award nomination in 1954 for his adapted score of *The Glenn Miller Story*.

Over the next few years, he scored and/or wrote songs for dozens of movies, but it was a side project for television that brought him the greatest attention. Blake Edwards asked Mancini to write the score for a new detective series, *Peter Gunn*. The resulting theme music remains one of television's most famous background scores. It also ensured the success of the series, by Blake Edwards's own admission, and won Mancini the award for Best Instrumental Arrangement and Album of the Year at the very first Grammy Awards that year, 1958.

> **Q.** Mancini won another Grammy two years later for another Blake Edwards series. What was its name?
>
> **A.** *Mr. Lucky*, which won for Best Arrangement.

Taking new note of Mancini, Hollywood responded by awarding him the Oscar for Best Musical Score for *Breakfast at Tiffany's* (1961), as well as the Best Song Oscar for "Moon River" from the same movie, with lyrics by Johnny Mercer. On top of that, the title track for the film *Bachelor in Paradise*, with lyrics by Mack David, was also nominated for an Oscar. No one was in the least surprised when "Moon River" also picked up Grammys for Record of the Year, Song of the Year, and Arrangement of the Year.

Mancini teamed up with Johnny Mercer again to take the Best Song Oscar for the second year in a row for "Days of Wine and Roses." The song went on to win Grammys for Record of the Year and Song of the Year. Blake Edwards had directed both *Breakfast at Tiffany's* and *Days of Wine and Roses*, and down through the years there would be many more Edwards pictures that would bring Mancini either Best Score or Best Song Oscar nominations: *The Pink Panther* (1964), *The Great Race* (1965), *Darling Lili* (1970), *The Pink Panther Strikes Again* (1976), *10* (1979), and *Victor, Victoria* (1982), for which Mancini won his fourth Oscar, for Best Score.

But Mancini always remained in great demand by other directors, too, and he responded with scintilating scores or songs for movies as different as *An Officer and a Gentleman* (1982), *The Glass Menagerie* (1987), and 1990's *Born on the Fourth of July*. There have been quite a lot of bad movies along the way, inevitably, but even when the movie itself has been a dud, the critics have often said something to the effect that the film in question "wastes a fine Henry Mancini score." The composer is only in his mid-sixties, still very much in demand, and it seems entirely likely that he is not yet through collecting Oscars and Grammys for his always evocative music.

A Drive to Win

●━●━●━●━●━●━●━●━●━●━●━●━●━●━●━●━●

ALTHOUGH HE BECAME PERHAPS the most legendary coach in the history of professional football, Vince Lombardi did not become a head coach until surprisingly late in life. That was not because he was a late bloomer, but because he was a man of fresh vision and a determination to resist the blandishments of the title Head Coach unless it carried the power to completely shape a team.

Born on July 11, 1913, in the Sheepshead Bay section of Brooklyn, where his immigrant father had become a successful butcher, Lombardi's academic abilities were on a par with his talent as a football player. From Brooklyn's St. Francis Prep he went on to Fordham University, where he played football under Jim Crowley, one of Notre Dame's famous "Four Horsemen." He then took a law degree at Fordham while playing football on weekends with the semipro Wilmington Clippers. There were a number of possible career paths open to him, but his love of football led him to take a job coaching at St. Cecilia High School in Engelwood, New Jersey, as well as teaching subjects ranging from Latin to algebra.

At St. Cecilia's he began experimenting with the T-formation, then regarded as a radical departure, and coached his team to thirty-two victories without a loss and earned the state championship. He attracted notice and was offered the head coaching job at his alma mater, Fordham. He turned down the position, though, feeling that he would not have enough authority to build the kind of team he wanted. Two years later, in 1949, he took the head coaching job at West Point, but as he was beginning to make real headway, the team was decimated by a cheating scandal. He was successful enough, though, to finally be offered an offensive coach's job with the 1954 New York Giants. The Giants were in the championship game in both 1956 and 1958, winning the first and losing the second. There were feelers about becoming head coach at more than one team, but as had been the case with Fordham, he felt that he would not have enough authority. It was Lombardi's desire to serve as both general manager and head coach, so that he would have complete control over personnel decisions.

By 1959, the once-mighty Green Bay Packers were in such pitiful shape that they gave him what he wanted, and the beginning of a legendary dynasty was put in place. He coached the team to a winning season in his first year and began grooming two young players, quarterback Bart Starr and running back Paul Hornung, for greatness. The following year, Green Bay became division champions for the first time in sixteen years and was named the Comeback Team of the Year, while Lombardi himself was named Coach of the Year. In both 1961 and 1962, Green Bay won the National Football League championship game against the New York Giants. When Paul Hornung was suspended for a year for betting on games—though not Packer games—the Packers did not reach the championship game until 1966, which they won against Cleveland. The next two seasons climaxed with Superbowls I and II, both of which Green Bay won against Kansas City and then Oakland.

Ready for new challenges, Lombardi moved over to the

faltering Washington Redskins for the 1969 season, and led the team to a winning season. Now ill, he made a final pre-season pilgrimage to the Redskins' locker-room, and passed away a few days later on September 4, 1970, at the age of fifty-seven.

Lombardi was a tough coach who gave players he did not think were living up to their abilities a hard time. There were always some who couldn't take it, but there were many more who credited him with turning them into the stars they became. They revered him, and his toughness seemed to touch a deep American nerve in the turbulent 1960s. "I'm not a second-place man," he said, and even more famously—at least in the recollections of others following his death—"Winning isn't everything, it's the only thing." There was no question he knew how to win and how to inspire others to give their very best.

Undefeated

‚ñ†‚ñ†‚ñ†‚ñ†‚ñ†‚ñ†‚ñ†‚ñ†‚ñ†‚ñ†‚ñ†‚ñ†‚ñ†‚ñ†‚ñ†‚ñ†‚ñ†‚ñ†‚ñ†

THE SHOEMAKER'S SON FROM Brockton, Massachusetts, wanted to be a major-league baseball player. But when Rocco Francis Marchegiano finally got a major-league tryout at the age of twenty-three in 1946, it was a disaster. He dropped balls, fell all over himself, and was sternly advised to forget about a baseball career.

As a serviceman during World War II, he had done a little boxing, so he decided to try his hand at that sport as a professional, and changed his name to Rocky Marciano. Hands, fast and powerful, were in fact the only thing he had going for him at first; he looked as ungainly stumbling around a ring as he had behind the plate as a catcher. Boxing fans laughed at him—but nobody could beat him. He got real respect for the first time when he beat Joe Louis in 1951.

On September 23, 1952, in Philadelphia, Marciano took the world championship from Jersey Joe Walcott. For the next four years, Marciano reigned supreme, turning back all comers. He won all forty-nine fights he had fought as a professional, forty-three with knockouts. Then he did something that great athletes and great singers seldom have the sense or willpower

*Rocky Marciano laying a pulverizing punch to one of his un-
lucky opponents* ARCHIVE PHOTOS

to do. At the height of his fame, and the peak of his abilities, he retired from the ring for good. Many people tried to lure him back, but he refused to be tempted. As a result, he stands in the record books as the only heavyweight champion never to be defeated.

Game Master

•❤•❤•❤•❤•❤•❤•❤•❤•❤•❤•❤•❤•❤•❤•

IT SEEMED AS THOUGH the American GI during World War II was constantly being instructed about something. GIs never knew what it was going to be next, from foxhole digging to venereal disease, but it was always something.

There was one bit of education that was always a hit with the soldiers at army camps in the United States and Europe. The civilian instructor, a suave man in his early forties, always had the soldiers mesmerized in minutes. What was he teaching them? How to spot card cheats and loaded dice.

The instructor was John Scarne, born March 4, 1903, and destined to become the greatest expert on the planet on the subject of games and gambling. He was bamboozling the folks in Steubenville, Ohio, with palmed quarters and card tricks before he was out of short pants. But even as a young man, Scarne wasn't interested in taking a sucker for a ride; he was interested in the *science* of games of chance. He wrote countless books on games and gambling, and served as a consultant to organizations ranging from hotel chains to the FBI. His particular love was for the endless permutations of the game of bridge, and his syndicated column on the game was a fixture in newspapers around the world for decades.

He spent his life trying to give the sucker an even break, for once, by exposing the tricks of professional card sharks. His hobby, he once said, was "fooling other magicians." A man of wit and charm, Scarne spent a long, rich life playing games—very seriously—and died on July 5, 1985.

Coddling the Stars

●▬●▬●▬●▬●▬●▬●▬●▬●▬●▬●▬●▬●

> **Q.** Name the only restaurateur ever to win a Tony Award.
>
> **A.** Who else but Vincent Sardi, Jr., whose special Tony was presented to him at the very first Tony Award ceremony in 1947, for "providing the best transient home and haven" for show people.

AN INSTITUTION IN THE heart of New York's theater district, on West Forty-fourth Street, Sardi's was never a mecca for gourmets or gourmands, but its ambiance has attracted untold numbers of tourists, as well as New Yorkers, charmed by the caricatures of generations of Broadway stars that line its walls. For decades, the restaurant was *the* place for opening-night parties, held on the second floor (although the stars would generally make a grand entrance to the applause of customers and eat their postperformance supper on the first floor before joining the anxious wait for the reviews upstairs).

The restaurant was originally opened by Vincent Sardi, Sr., who had emigrated from Italy, but it was Vincent junior who did the most to make it into a Broadway legend. Born on July 23, 1915, he went to Columbia University as a premed student, but was quickly enticed into the family business, "taking care of people in a different way," as he has put it. Famous for his generosity to actors on their way up or down on their luck, Vincent Sardi's big smile, warm welcome, and genuine love of the theater world reflect a man who has never seen a performance or a play he couldn't find a kind word for. Convivial and gregarious in a way that bespeaks his heritage, Sardi has always had the heart of a fan and the soul of a perfect host.

The Singing
Shakespearean

●▬●▬●▬●▬●▬●▬●▬●▬●▬●▬●▬●▬●

W IDELY REGARDED AS THE greatest Broadway singer/actor
of the twentieth century, Alfred Drake electrified audiences in Rodgers and Hammerstein's *Oklahoma!* in 1943,
Cole Porter's biggest hit, *Kiss Me, Kate,* in 1948, and in 1953,
Kismet, based on the music of Alexander Borodin.

Even when he appeared in a flop show, his notices were
invariably raves. But he regarded himself as a classical actor,
and often turned down musical roles to do much less well-
paid work acting in Shakespearean plays and directing other
dramas from the classic repertoire. Asked to play the king in
The King and I, he demanded a salary of five thousand dollars
a week—an unheard-of amount then—as a ploy to get out of
doing his expected singing role. Two years later, however, he
was paid that amount for *Kismet,* and turned the show into
one more personal triumph and a considerable hit.

Born Alfredo Capurro on October 7, 1914 in the Bronx,
he became smitten with Shakespeare's work at Brooklyn College under the tutelage of the important Shakespearean scholar
Bernard Grebanier. He was an accomplished Shakespearean
actor and often worked with other great figures, playing Bene-
dick to Katharine Hepburn's Beatrice in *Much Ado About
Nothing* and Claudius to Richard Burton's *Hamlet.* But when

he combined his superb acting abilities with the great power and buttery tones of his baritone singing voice, audiences went away knowing that they had seen the very best. Despite being rather short in stature, Drake gave the impression of enormous authority. When he strode across the Broadway stage in one of his musicals, he seemed to command the world.

The young crooner Frank Sinatra keeping his legions of fans happy at an autograph session with Louella Parsons
ARCHIVE PHOTOS

Not Just a Song
to Sing

●▬●▬●▬●▬●▬●▬●▬●▬●▬●▬●▬●▬●▬●▬●▬●

V ERY FEW ENTERTAINERS HAVE had megastar careers as both
Hollywood icons and as concert singers, the three most
notable being Judy Garland, Marlene Dietrich, and Frank
Sinatra. Of the three, Garland was the most loved, Dietrich
the most glamorous, and Sinatra the most successful. What
makes Sinatra's story so interesting is that it all seems more
than a little unlikely.

An extremely skinny kid with big ears from Hoboken, New
Jersey, who started out wanting to be a sportswriter, Sinatra
was born to a boilermaker from Catania, Sicily (whose name
had been anglicized to Martin) and his wife, Dolly, christened
Natalie, from Genoa. Martin eventually got a job as a fireman,
thanks in large part to the efforts of Dolly, who was Democratic
precinct captain with a good deal of political clout. Francis
Albert Sinatra was born on December 12, 1915, but his early
show-biz bios stated his birth date as two years later—the better
to capitalize on his very youthful appearance.

Sinatra took the quartet route of thousands of other young
singers, initially appearing with a local group called the Hoboken Four and then moving on to solo gigs at lower-echelon
vaudeville houses. But 1939 found him working at an Engle-
wood, New Jersey, roadhouse called the Rustic Cabin, where

he sang a few songs and acted as emcee for the nightly shows. Into this byway walked the great bandleader Harry James. James thought Sinatra looked "like a wet rag," but he knew a wonderful voice when he heard one and hired Sinatra on the spot to tour with his band. Less than a year later, a magnanimous James let Sinatra out of his contract to take a better deal from Tommy Dorsey. He went over in a big way from the start. Six singles with the Dorsey band made the Top Ten on *Billboard*'s singles chart in 1940, including "I'll Never Smile Again" and "Stardust."

Sinatra stayed with Dorsey until September 1942. During that period he also made his first two movies as part of the Dorsey band, *Las Vegas Nights* and *Ship Ahoy*. When he left Dorsey to go solo, Dorsey retained financial rights to over 40 percent of Sinatra's income and it was years before Sinatra managed to buy Dorsey out. Trying to go it alone was risky—only Bing Crosby had truly succeeded—but his first solo appearance, as an added attraction with Benny Goodman's band in December 1942 at New York's Paramount Theater, caused such an eruption from the audience that Goodman nearly jumped out of his skin. It was clear Sinatra could make it on his own.

Part of Sinatra's success in the 1940s was based on his sex appeal with "bobby-soxers," who screamed and swooned for "Frankie" as they later would for Elvis and the Beatles. But he worked hard to develop an adult following as well, singing at nightclubs and even with symphony orchestras. For adults it was the way Sinatra sang, not his physical presence, that was the basis of his appeal. The great technical developments in microphones, fueled by sound movies, allowed Sinatra to sing in a more intimate and lyrical way than would have been possible if he had started out a decade earlier. He also perfected several tricks of breathing—some of them gleaned from Dorsey's trumpet playing—that gave him a remarkably seamless sound. Perhaps most important of all, Sinatra had an instinctive genius for musical interpretation and word phrasing that made him almost a collaborator with the composer and lyricist. It is difficult for many people to grasp fifty years later, but nobody had ever before sung popular songs quite the way he did. It was a new kind of sound.

The 1940s were good to Sinatra. There were more hit singles, legendary concert dates (including one that caused a riot among the thirty thousand people waiting to get in to hear him perform between movie showings at New York's Paramount), and more and more starring roles in movies. The best of these were his three efforts with Gene Kelly, *Anchors Aweigh* (1945), *Take Me Out to the Ball Game* (1949), and the classic *On the Town* (1949). Sinatra turned out to be a remarkably good dancer, and managed to pretty much hold his own with Kelly, but the movies without him were never as successful— some of them, such as 1948's *The Kissing Bandit*, were close to being disasters.

The bad movies he made were having an effect on his popularity, and a new generation of teenagers were looking for new young singers to swoon over. He was getting a great deal of bad press because of his tempestuous affair with Ava Gardner, which led to his divorce from his first wife, childhood sweetheart Nancy Barbato, whom he had married in 1939 and who had borne him three children. His marriage to Gardner in November 1951 did not quiet things down; Frank and Ava seemed to have more fights than any couple in Hollywood, and a great many of them were in public and made the headlines. Then his voice gave out. He was dropped by his record label, Columbia, and his agent, powerful MCA. It looked as though he might be through.

Sinatra had read James Jones's controversial best-seller *From*

Here to Eternity and was certain he was the one and only absolutely right actor to play the spunky but pitiful soldier Maggio, who is beaten to death. Columbia studio head Harry Cohn wasn't so sure, but he was always looking for people to hire on the cheap. He got a desperate, begging Sinatra extremely cheap—eight thousand dollars—but the deal paid off for Sinatra in a big way. He gave a powerfully haunting performance that won him high critical praise, audience favor, and a slew of awards, including the Oscar for Best Supporting Actor of 1953.

Sinatra was back in Hollywood favor, his voice was back in full force, and a new 1954 recording contract with Capitol brought him one top-selling album after another over the next seven years, after which he switched labels to Reprise with almost equal success. He won high praise in movies as diverse as *The Man with the Golden Arm* (1955), for which he was nominated as Best Actor, *High Society* (1956), *Some Came Running* (1958), and *The Manchurian Candidate* (1962). There were a lot of less memorable films, including several with members of Hollywood's famous Rat Pack (Dean Martin, Sammy Davis, Jr., Peter Lawford, and Shirley MacLaine among them), but they did just fine at the box office.

Separated from Ava Gardner in 1953, and finally divorced in 1957, Sinatra was connected romantically with a long list of Hollywood's female stars. He married twenty-year-old Mia Farrow in 1966—but the union lasted less than two years. Ten years later he married Barbara Marx and finally achieved a settled relationship. With his romantic liaisons, occasional fistfights, and rumored Mafia connections, Sinatra has seldom managed to stay out of the tabloids for long, but he has also done a great deal of charitable work, including helping down-on-their-luck old friends, almost always anonymously. Even with his anonymity, Hollywood knew how generous he had been with so many and awarded him the prestigious Jean Hersholt Humanitarian Award in 1988.

And the man has gone on singing, drawing vast numbers of fans to hear him one more time, often in Las Vegas, but also on cross-country tours with various other major stars, including Liza Minnelli and, in 1992, his old pal Shirley MacLaine. The voice may not have as much sheen, but critics have cheered his continued ability to create moments of intense magic even in theaters as vast as New York's Radio City Music Hall. Drawing on a lifetime of emotional resonance, and the unique style he has honed over a half century, Sinatra has never lost the knack of making a listener feel that a song is being sung just to that one person.

Rockets to the Moon

●▬●▬●▬●▬●▬●▬●▬●▬●▬●▬●▬●▬●▬●▬●▬●

WHEN THE LUNAR MODULE from *Apollo 11*, carrying Neil Armstrong and Buzz Aldrin, landed on the surface of the moon on July 20, 1969, not even the two pioneering astronauts themselves could have been more elated than their boss back on earth, the Italian-American director of Apollo launch operations, Rocco A. Petrone. Petrone had been with the Apollo program from its inception, first as managing director of the building program and then as director of launch operations beginning in 1966. In 1961, when President Kennedy called for landing a man on the moon within a decade, the fledgling program that Petrone had taken charge of the previous year suddenly went into high gear—and, despite much public and scientific skepticism that the task could be accomplished, Rocco Petrone was one of those who was absolutely convinced that the goal was feasible, needing only the proper allotment of national resources.

Petrone, born on March 31, 1926, in Amsterdam, New York, had been fascinated with space travel since his boyhood. Upon his graduation from the Massachusetts Institute of Technology in 1952, he went directly to a job as a development officer at the Redstone Missile Development base in Huntsville, Alabama. Four years later he became a member of the

Army General Staff in Washington, and then moved on to the Apollo program in 1960. He was only thirty-four years old at the time, but there was no question among either the Pentagon brass or rocket scientists that he was the man for the job. A first-rate scientific mind, a real gift for administration, and an ability to generate enthusiasm among a diverse mix of military officers, civilian scientists, and aerospace manufacturers were called for, and he had them all.

Nothing would test Petrone more seriously than the tragic explosion and fire as *Apollo 7* stood on its launching pad at the Kennedy Space Center in Florida in January 1967, killing the three astronauts aboard for tests. But Petrone rallied his forces and, only twenty-three months later, *Apollo 8* made the first voyage around the moon and back. Nine months later, the words came back from *Apollo 11* on the surface of the moon, "Tranquility Base here. The *Eagle* has landed."

Mission accomplished, Petrone moved to Washington to oversee the Apollo program in its entirety, serving from 1969 to 1973 as its overall director. After a year as director of the Marshall Space Flight Center in Huntsville, Alabama, he spent another year as the associate director of NASA. From 1975 to 1981 he was the chief executive officer of the National Center for Resource Recovery, and then joined Rockwell International, where he became president of the company's Space Transportation and Systems Group in 1982.

His career was distinguished all around, but Rocco Petrone can claim a success that no one else can or ever will be able to claim: He was in charge of launching from this planet the first human beings ever to set foot on another celestial body.

Automobile Man

●━●━●━●━●━●━●━●━●━●━●━●━●━●━●━●━●

THE AMERICAN PUBLIC GOT its first major introduction to
Lee Iacocca in 1964 when, in conjunction with the debut
of the Ford Mustang, Iacocca managed to get himself featured
on the covers of both *Time* and *Newsweek*. He was then the
general manager of the Ford Motor Company, having worked
his way rapidly up the ladder from an initial job with the field
sales staff in 1946. By 1970, he would be president of the
company, but those two magazine covers in 1964 would sow
the first seeds of an increasing jealousy and distrust on the part
of company owner Henry Ford II. Ford had not been enthu-
siastic about the Mustang, but Iacocca had been convinced
that it would far exceed the initial sales projection of one
hundred thousand cars. It in fact more than quadrupled that
figure, which further fed the rivalry between the two men and
at the same time made Iacocca more powerful.

Lido Anthony Iacocca was born in Allentown, Pennsylvania, on October 15, 1924, the son of an Italian immigrant
who built himself a very successful business in hot-dog res-
taurants, movie theaters, and rental cars, only to lose everything during the Depression, and then gain it back, and then
some, in real estate and contracting. As the only son, Lee
Iacocca was driven to live up to and surpass his father's stan-

dards of success. He attended Lehigh University and then took an engineering degree at Princeton and went straight to work for Ford.

Following up on the Mustang, Iacocca introduced the Maverick, the Thunderbird, and the Pinto, among other successes, and was at the height of his powers when Henry Ford II decided that he had had enough, convinced that Iacocca planned to usurp the company from Ford family ownership. In 1978, Henry Ford II fired the man who had been responsible for fourteen years of Ford ascendance.

Iacocca was by then a very wealthy man, and with the compensation coming to him from Ford as a part of his leaving, he could have easily retired then and there. But Iacocca was too ambitious for that, and when the beleagured Chrysler Corporation approached him to become its president and chief operating officer, he could not resist. In the fall of 1978 he took over at Chrysler, believing that the company could be turned around by the K-cars then on the drawing boards. But Chrysler turned out to be in far worse shape than he had realized, both financially and in terms of a decaying manufacturing ability.

The answer, he soon realized, lay only in a United States Government loan of one and a half billion dollars. It was a bruising fight that forced Iacocca to stifle his well-known temper and humble himself before Congress. But he managed to convince Congress, President Carter, and through an immensely skillful presentation, the public, that allowing Chrysler to go under would cause disastrous effects on the economy of the country as a whole, including massive rises in unemployment. The loan went through, and he began the job of bringing Chrysler back from the precipice, doing it so effectively that the company was able to repay the government loan with a single check in 1983, seven years ahead of schedule.

He had been elected chairman of the board, while continuing as chief executive officer in 1979, and with the repayment, he came to be regarded as one of the great geniuses in American corporate history. This reputation was further fueled by his 1984 book, *Iacocca: An Autobiography*, which became one of the all-time nonfiction best-sellers. Back on the cover of *Time* in 1985, the focus now was not just on his automotive genius but the possibility of his candidacy for president of the United States. He wouldn't say yes to that, but he said no in a way that kept the possibility in the air through the 1988 election and beyond.

Iacocca has his detractors as well as his defenders, but he has become the most visible corporate leader of his time, in no small part due to his personal television advertising pitches for Chrysler cars. Ironically, he is a shy man who hates television, and it took him an enormous effort of will to create the television image so familiar to Americans. A complex man of many great gifts, he has managed in some ways to remain a slightly mysterious figure, larger than life but not entirely knowable. There is no question, though, that he has become one of the foremost figures of his time.

Faster, Fastest

●━●━●━●━●━●━●━●━●━●━●━●━●━●━●━●━●

L EGENDARY RACE-CAR DRIVER MARIO Gabriel Andretti, born in Montona, Italy, on February 28, 1940, came to the United States when he was fifteen, his family settling in Pennsylvania. At his high school a girl named Dee Ann Hoch tutored him in English. They became sweethearts and were married in 1961, the same year that Andretti began his long and still-active career as a professional race-car driver. He moved up fast in the driver's ranks, and by 1965 was making his first start in the biggest race of them all, the Indianapolis 500. He had a terrific race that year, qualifying in fourth place and moving up to third at the finish, more than enough to gain him Rookie of the Year honors.

After that auspicious start, though, the next several years at Indianapolis turned into disasters. In 1966, he finished eighteenth, after starting in the pole position; gaining the pole position again in 1967, the finish was far worse, with a lost wheel pushing him back to thirtieth place. The next two years piston problems took his cars out of action and pushed him back to thirty-third place (dead last) although he had been favored to win. He had won two national championships and set speed records at tracks all across the country, but he seemed to be jinxed at the Indianapolis 500.

Determined to win in 1969, he bought a radical new Lotus design—only to have it burn in a qualifying-race crash that left him with painful first- and second-degree burns on his face. Never one to give up, Andretti qualified in second position using a backup Ford-Brawner Hawk. It was a race plagued by minor problems with his car that always seemed on the verge of taking him out of the race once again. But in the end, the car held up, other drivers who were ahead of him were hit by the Indy jinx, and he cruised in the winner. He had led the race for 116 of the 200 laps, and established fifteen new records in the course of it.

Andretti was the overall Indianapolis Speedway Champion in 1965, 1966, 1969, and 1984. He was national Driver of the Year in 1976, 1978, and 1984, Dirt Track Champion in 1974, and the Formula One World Champion in 1978. But he still considers the 1969 Indianapolis 500 win his most important race—not least because he has been unable to win it again, despite top starting positions year after year. His sons Michael and Jeff have also become top drivers and are themselves trying to win the elusive Indy. All three raced in the 1992 500. Mario and Jeff both ended up in the hospital after crashes, and Michael's engine died as he was leading by a wide margin with only eleven laps to go. But the day may yet come for the Andretti sons.

Making Movies
His Way

●▬●▬●▬●▬●▬●▬●▬●▬●▬●▬●▬●▬●

I N 1971, B-MOVIE KING ROGER Corman hired a twenty-nine-year-old director with one low-budget feature to his credit to direct a contemporary Bonnie-and-Clyde story called *Boxcar Bertha*. It starred a young actress who would go on to become one of Hollywood's most respected performers. During the filming, the actress gave the director a copy of the Nikos Kazantzakis novel *The Last Temptation of Christ*. The actress was Barbara Hershey and the director was Martin Scorsese. Sixteen years later, Scorsese would finally make a movie of *The Last Temptation of Christ*, for which he would receive an Oscar nomination as Best Director, featuring Barbara Hershey as Mary Magdalene.

This kind of strong connection between actor and director has been typical of Martin Scorsese's career, and so has a high degree of controversy, which reached its apex with *The Last Temptation of Christ*. The movie was picketed by a number of religious groups on the grounds that it was blasphemous—although it turned out that a lot of the picketers had never seen the film. The controversy was ironic in that as a young man Scorsese had started out attending New York City's Cathedral College as a seminarian, and his films have often been cited by critics for their strong themes of sin and redemption.

Born November 17, 1942, Scorsese grew up in Manhattan's
Little Italy. Transferring from Cathedral College to New York
University, he went on to earn a master's degree in the university's renowned film program. He completed several short
films and then directed his first feature on a shoestring budget.
The movie *Who's That Knocking at My Door?*, starring a
young Harvey Keitel—who would make several more films
with the director—was shown at the Chicago Film Festival in
1967, but was not released until 1969. Scorsese then worked
as one of the editors on *Woodstock* before making *Mean Streets*,
based on his own story about the Little Italy in which he had
grown up. Starring Harvey Keitel and Robert De Niro—in the
first of many collaborations—the 1973 movie immediately
marked him with critics as an important young director.

His next movie, *Alice Doesn't Live Here Anymore*, which
brought a 1974 Best Actress Oscar to Ellen Burstyn and a
Supporting Actress nomination for Diane Ladd, suggested,
despite some quirkiness, that Scorsese was moving into the
Hollywood mainstream. But his next extremely controversial
movie, 1976's *Taxi Driver*, turned back toward the gritty dark-
ness of *Mean Streets*. There were a lot of objections to the
extreme violence of the film's ending, and a good deal of
scandalized muttering about Jodie Foster's fourteen-year-old
prostitute, but the movie was nominated for Best Picture, Foster for Best Supporting Actress, and star Robert De Niro as
Best Actor. Scorsese himself did not get a Best Director nomination—Hollywood was clearly confused about what kind of
artist he really was.

His next three efforts confused everybody even further:
American Boy (1977), a quasidocumentary fifty-five-minute
portrait of his friend Steven Prince; *New York, New York* (1977)
starring Liza Minelli and De Niro in a splashy musical that
was also a downer; and *The Last Waltz* (1978), a delirious and

riveting documentary of the final performance of the rock group The Band. All three left open the question: Who is Martin Scorsese?

For many critics, the answer seemed to come with 1980's *Raging Bull*, a stunningly filmed black-and-white biography of the boxer Jake La Motta. A dozen years later many critics regard this as one of the finest films ever made, but there are strong dissenters and it was a box-office flop. It did bring Scorsese his first nomination as Best Director, and six other nominations, including Best Picture, but only the Film Editing and Robert De Niro's starring performance won Oscars.

Admittedly stung by his loss of the Oscar to first-time director Robert Redford, Scorsese's next two movies seemed deliberately "in-your-face" efforts. Neither the sour *King of Comedy* (1983) nor the quirky *After Hours* (1985) were successes with either critics or audiences. Then in 1986 came a solid hit with *The Color of Money*, a sequel to the classic poolhall movie of twenty-five years earlier, *The Hustler*. But Hollywood appeared to think that the movie owed its success to the pairing of Paul Newman, who won the Best Actor Oscar in a reprise of the pool-shark role he had first been nominated for a quarter-century before, and the hottest new star in town, Tom Cruise. Scorsese was not even nominated for Best Director.

The Oscar nomination he received in 1988 for *The Last Temptation of Christ* seemed largely motivated by a Hollywood antipathy to the attempted censorship efforts surrounding the movie. But Scorsese demonstrated his enormous abilities again in 1990 with the mob movie *Goodfellas*. The old hard edge was there, as well as some hilariously grim comedy, and the critics couldn't find enough superlatives to heap on the movie. But it lost the Best Picture Oscar to the daring—but much more congenial—epic *Dances with Wolves*, whose star, Kevin

Costner, became the second first-time director to trump Scorsese. He came right back in 1991 with a remake of the 1962 thriller *Cape Fear* that audiences flocked to but critics felt was well below his best work.

The question remains: Will Martin Scorsese ever put it all together with a box-office hit that the critics call great and Hollywood will reward with a shower of Oscars? Or does it really matter—neither Alfred Hitchcock nor Orson Welles ever got an Oscar for directing, but their movies will last as long as there are screens to show them on, a destiny that seems certain for Martin Scorsese's finest achievements.

Shaping the Canvas

•◆•◆•◆•◆•◆•◆•◆•◆•◆•◆•◆•◆•

F EW AMERICAN ARTISTS OF any time have had such immediate and early success as Frank Stella, born in Malden,
Massachusetts, in 1936. Even as a prep-school student at Phillips Academy, Andover, the artist and painting instructor Pat
Morgan knew he was teaching a boy destined for immense
success—someone, in fact, who did not really need teaching,
since he already had a mature vision and the technical abilities
to express it. Stella went on to Princeton University, but left
to settle in New York in 1958. In 1960, at the age of twenty-
four, he had his first solo exhibition at the famous Leo Castelli
Gallery in New York City, and was viewed by critics and
collectors as an important new painter. In a period when Abstract Expressionism still reigned supreme in the American art
world, his large, brilliantly colored, "hard-edged" paintings
making use of interlocking geometrical forms were still abstract
but in a less overtly emotional and personal way. At a very
young age, he had found a visual language that was uniquely
his own.

His paintings were not only admired, but sold. They were
a perfect match for the vast lobbies of the corporate office
buildings being built at the time—a Stella painting was not
easily overwhelmed. Private art collectors had begun acquiring

his work early, and museums soon followed suit. No major museum featuring modern art can consider its collection complete without a Stella. Early paintings are now worth millions of dollars, and his new works have made him one of the wealthiest artists of our time. But despite his financial success, he has not rested on his laurels, simply repeating past successes. In the early 1970s and again in the mid-1980s, he stepped back and took the time he needed to reconfigure his vision. His work was the subject of a major touring show organized by the Museum of Modern Art in 1987, when he was only fifty-one. He shows every sign of being able to continue to develop in fresh and sometimes surprising ways. Early success often fizzles out, but that has certainly not been the case with Frank Stella.

Reconfiguring
Human Spaces

•◦•◦•◦•◦•◦•◦•◦•◦•◦•◦•◦•◦•◦•

"PICTURESQUE MEDIOCRE SLIME," ONE irate British critic said of the new addition to London's National Gallery that opened in 1991. Cooler and wiser heads have prevailed, however, and the building has come to be regarded as a triumph: "There hasn't been a gentler public building put up in London since Sir Christopher Wren," Paul Goldberger of *The New York Times* wrote a year later. But it is doubtful that the American architect Robert Venturi was either surprised or disturbed by some of the initial criticism. Time and again over the past thirty years buildings designed by Venturi have had brickbats thrown at them to start with, only to become accepted as masterful creations within a surprisingly short period of time.

Why all the controversy? The first paragraph of Romaldo Giurgola's entry on Venturi in the massive reference book *Contemporary Architects* tells a lot of the story. "Robert Venturi is presently one of the most original talents in contemporary architecture in the United States," writes Giurgola. " . . . his projects and writings provide a critical, underlying strength for the alternatives to the American functionalism that developed in the late 1950s. He has also been instrumental in devising an architecture that has its counterpart in the Pop movement in the figurative arts."

Words like *original, alternative,* and *Pop movement* are like red flags to conservative curators of the status quo. Something new and different? God forbid. Such critics always manage to forget that there was a time when the Parthenon and Gothic cathedrals and glass skyscrapers were also something new. Time moves on, and Robert Venturi has been from the start a leader in expressing a new age in architecture. Ironically, one of the things that so upsets his critics is that he has forged a new vision by incorporating old decorative themes that had been discarded by the stripped-down but massive buildings so favored as corporate headquarters. Among many other qualities, Venturi's buildings have a sense of fun—and there are always those to complain that fun means unserious.

Robert Venturi, born in Philadelphia on June 25, 1925, has always been serious about his work. A summa cum laude 1947 graduate of Princeton, where he also took his Master of Fine Arts degree, he has been an extremely influential professor of architecture at both the University of Pennsylvania and Yale. With a series of partners, he has headed his own architectural firm in Philadelphia since 1958, now called Venturi, Rauch, and Scott Brown. His work—often in collaboration with his wife since 1967, Denise Scott Brown—has been noteworthy for its sensitivity to social conditions and locale, scaled to human use and enjoyment.

Among Venturi's best-known buildings are a number of private houses, including several on Nantucket; the Humanities Building at the State University of New York at Purchase; Gordon Wu Hall at Princeton; Franklin Court in Philadelphia; the Seattle Art Museum; and Orchestra Hall in Philadelphia. His writing on architecture, much of it done in collaboration with his wife, is required reading in the profession, and his influence among younger architects grows steadily.

A man with a capacity for seeing things freshly and the talent to carry a vision to fruition, Venturi has become one of the foremost figures of his time in the world of architecture.

A Monumental Task

●▬●▬●▬●▬●▬●▬●▬●▬●▬●▬●▬●▬●

For TWENTY-FIVE YEARS, FROM 1854 to 1879, he was perhaps the most ubiquitous presence in the long halls and high-ceilinged rooms of the United States Capitol Building in Washington, D.C. He was not a senator or a member of the House—those came and went over the years. Six different presidents occupied the White House. But he was always there at the seat of government, doing his painstaking work, a slight figure born in Rome, Italy, on July 26, 1805.

His name was Constantino Brumidi, and he was responsible for the painting of the innumerable murals and frescoes that are so much a part of the Capitol to this day. His talent had been recognized early in Italy, where he was given commissions by Pope Gregory XVI soon after the young artist graduated from the prestigious Academia San Lucca. Pius IX, who became pope in 1846, entrusted Brumidi with the restoration of some of the Vatican's Raphael frescoes, as well as commissioning two portraits of himself. After Brumidi supported the failed Garibaldi insurrection of 1848, Garibaldi fled to New York and urged Brumidi, who had been banished from Rome for life, to follow. In 1852, the artist made the journey and two years later was selected to paint some murals for the Capitol. He would continue the work over the next quarter-century, in spite of numerous objections by American-born artists. These complaints were not well founded—American artists were simply not schooled in fresco work, which presents great technical challenges. The technique involved pressing figure outlines into freshly applied plaster, and then painting the design in tempera while the plaster was still wet. It was a skill that had been refined over hundreds of years in Italy, but had very few American practitioners, and none with Brumidi's experience or artistic accomplishments. This was, after all, a man who had been entrusted with the restoration of murals by the revered Raphael.

Brumidi, working according to the wishes of Capitol architect T. U. Walter, began the seemingly endless work of decorating the miles of empty white walls of the vast complex. Among his most admired early successes were his work in the President's Room and the huge mural in the House chamber celebrating the surrender of Cornwallis to Washington at Yorktown. He worked on through the Civil War (Lincoln regarded the completion of the Capitol as a strong symbol that the Union would stand), and then in 1865 began his most difficult project, and the one that Americans are most familiar with: the interior of the great dome.

While the surface to be painted was only about half the size of the Sistine Chapel ceiling, Brumidi had to work nearly twice as far above the floor as had Michaelangelo. The Capitol scaffolding on which he lay rose at the center to one hundred and eighty feet, a lofty perch to which the sixty-year-old Brumidi was hoisted by a system of pulleys day after day for a year. That monumental task completed, Brumidi returned to less daunting work in other areas of the building. Then, in 1877, when he was seventy-two, he was asked to return aloft to paint the frieze of simulated statues that now surround the base of the dome. He had completed eight of the panels when a near fall in 1879 brought a halt to his work. His health deteriorated rapidly, and he died on February 19, 1880.

Brumidi's work was not on a par with the great Italian masters who had preceded him, and some of it was too sentimental or overblown to be taken entirely seriously. But he was as good as anyone of his time at what he did, and the finest of his achievements, including the dome, continue to impress vast numbers of visitors to Washington to this day.

Constantino Brumidi, who became a citizen of the United States in 1857, certainly left a legacy to his adopted country that is as striking a mixture of dedication to the ideals of America and the artistic heritage of his mother country as can be found.

The Congressman
from Newark

●━●━●━●━●━●━●━●━●━●━●━●━●━●━●━●━●

PETER WALLACE RODINO, JR., born in Newark, New Jersey, on June 7, 1909, had been in Congress for a quarter-century when he was thrust into the center of a maelstrom in late 1973. He had inherited the chairmanship of the House Judiciary Committee that year, due to his seniority, but he was regarded as an unassuming and not very important member of Congress by Washington standards. Now he was suddenly being called upon to chair the House proceedings on the impeachment of President Richard M. Nixon in the wake of the Watergate scandal.

The next few months would have tested anyone in his position to the limit, and as a man who had never craved the limelight, was small of stature, without charisma, and lacking any great rhetorical skill, there were those in Congress who shuddered at the thought of his trying to lead the Congress—and because the hearings were televised—the nation as a whole through the traumatic process of deciding whether or not to impeach a president of the United States for the first time in more than a hundred years. (Andrew Johnson, Lincoln's successor, had faced impeachment in the political turmoil following the Civil War, but had ultimately survived by one vote in the Senate.)

During the proceedings, Rodino was often accused by members of his own committee and the press of dragging his feet in confronting the endless stonewalling of the president's lawyers. But many members, even during the impeachment hearings, and many more afterward, came to believe that Rodino's cautious, methodical approach was in the end utterly essential to arriving at the eventual vote for impeachment in July of 1974. Here was no impetuous partisan, no rabble-rouser, no rush-to-judgment sort of man. Under enormous pressures, he led the committee with dignity and the occasionally necessary asperity. He had another quality that came through television sets into the living rooms of America: Rodino was a patriot, not of the tub-thumping kind who cried, "America, right or wrong," but of the old immigrant kind, a man who believed in the democratic ideals of the country his parents had immigrated to and the constitution that governed it.

The Teacher-Poet

●▬●▬●▬●▬●▬●▬●▬●▬●▬●▬●▬●▬●▬●▬●▬●

O NE OF THE OBITUARY notices for John Ciardi (June 24, 1916–March 30, 1986) began by calling him an "educator, lecturer, editor, critic, translator, and poet." But even this imposing list does not really do justice to his influence. The wider public knew him best from his weekly network radio program *Accent* from 1961 to 1962 and his appearances on National Public Radio in the 1980s, as well as his long tenure as the poetry editor of the *Saturday Review* from 1956 to 1972. He was also one of the best known and wittiest literary figures on the American lecture circuit, to which he devoted much of his time after 1961, following fifteen years as a professor at Harvard and then Rutgers.

But he also had wide influence in the literary life of the country as the director of the famous Bread Loaf Writers' Conference at Middlebury College each summer from 1955 to 1972. He was a fine critic, one of the rare ones whose high standards never turned him mean, and a much-admired poet in his own right. His poetry for children was especially widely read, and his 1959 textbook *How Does a Poem Mean?* has been regarded as a standard high school and college course book from the year of its publication.

A specialist in the roots of peculiarly American words, he

wrote A *Browser's Dictionary; and Native's Guide to the Unknown American Language,* a treasure trove of information on the uniqueness of the American language, in the last decade of his life. But his greatest achievement was without doubt his translation from the Renaissance Italian of Dante Alighieri's *Divine Comedy,* its three parts published from 1940 to 1970. Regarded as the most accurate and resonate yet approachable translation of Dante's masterpiece in our time, it brought Ciardi worldwide fame and continues to be the most widely read edition in the English language. He could hardly have done greater honor to the country of his forefathers.

A Man for All Seasons

●◆●◆●◆●◆●◆●◆●◆●◆●◆●◆●◆●◆●◆●

I T TAKES A VERY special kind of man to write equally well
about Edmund Spenser's Renaissance masterpiece *The Fa-
erie Queene* and the sport of baseball; to be both a superb,
much-cherished teacher and a highly regarded administrator,
to serve as president of one of the country's foremost universities and as baseball's National League president and eventually Commissioner of Baseball. It is even more remarkable
to achieve all these things and still be regarded—by all but a
few inevitable antagonists—as an exceptionally nice human
being. But all of these accomplishments seemed to come almost naturally to A. Bartlett Giamatti.

The son of a professor of Italian literature, he was born on
April 4, 1938, in Boston. Growing up in South Hadley, Mas-
sachusetts, he was an avid fan of the Boston Red Sox. After
graduating from Phillips Academy, Andover, he received his
B.A. at Yale, and went on to gain a Ph.D. in Comparative
Literature in 1964. He taught first at Princeton and then at
Yale, becoming a full professor in 1971. He was master of
Yale's Ezra Stiles College in the early 1970s and became the
surprise choice as president of Yale in 1978.

Over the next eight years, while retaining his professorship
in the English and comparative literature department, Gia-

matti managed to balance Yale's soaring budget, established
new lines of communication with both alumni and students,
and steered the university back toward a more traditional liberal
arts curriculum. Feeling that in these fast-moving times eight
years was enough for anyone to serve as a university president,
he announced his resignation.

Giamatti had always joked that all he had really wanted to
be was president of was baseball's American League. But it
was the National League that immediately snapped him up
for its presidency in 1986, which meant that his love for the
Red Sox would have to be more discretely held in the following
years. His two and a half years with the National League were
sufficiently impressive to make him a natural choice for the
job of Baseball Commissioner, to succeed Peter Ueberroth.
When he assumed the job in April 1989, he spoke to sportswriter Frank Delford about his feeling for the game and how
different people came to love it, saying that some people "come
to it through a love of statistics, or the smell of the glove, or
just for something that their grandfather recited to them when
they were very young. I keep saying: There are many routes
to the game. There are many routes to the kingdom of baseball."

Giamatti was instantly embroiled in the dispute over the
gambling case involving Cincinnati Reds manager Pete Rose,
which had begun to come to a boil even before the new
commissioner took office. Saddened to find himself pitted
against one of the greats of baseball, Giamatti nevertheless
took a tough stance in defense of the sanctity of the game.
Many applauded, but Pete Rose diehards were furious. Only
two weeks after the matter was finally settled with Rose's ex-
pulsion from the game for life, Giamatti suddenly died of a
heart attack at his summer home on Martha's Vineyard on
September 1, 1989. He was fifty-one years old. Fans, even

those angry about the Rose case, were stunned. Even then Yankee owner George Steinbrenner wept, despite his rancorous relationship with Giamatti.

Fifty-one is a very young age to die, but Bart Giamatti had already lived enough for two or three men. Author of several distinguished books on literature, he had been the recipient of honorary degrees from numerous universities, received the Order of Merit of both Italy and West Germany, and France's National Order of Arts and Letters. He left behind a wife and three grown children, a legion of friends, and vast numbers of admirers to whom he had come no closer than to sit in the same baseball stadium on a sunny summer afternoon watching the game he loved.

A Cowboy Detective

●▬●▬●▬●▬●▬●▬●▬●▬●▬●▬●▬●▬●▬●▬●

IN 1885, THE FIRST AUTOBIOGRAPHICAL account of cowboy life appeared, called A *Texas Cowboy, or, Fifteen Years on the Hurricane Deck of a Spanish Pony*. It was a sensation, running through printing after printing and selling hundreds of thousands of copies. This remarkable volume was written by an Italian American, Charles Angelo Siringo, whose immigrant father had settled in Matagorda County, Texas.

Born on February 7, 1855, Charley Siringo began herding cattle when he was sixteen years old, going from Texas along the famed Chisholm Trail to such Kansas cattle-shipping towns as Abilene, Ellsworth, and Dodge City. Working for "Shanghai" Pierce or Beals and Bates, who had a vast ranch in the panhandle, Siringo experienced every aspect of cowboy life from stampedes to fighting off rustlers, not to mention riding in posses chasing Billy the Kid.

Tiring of the rigors of the trail, he settled down as a storekeeper in Caldwell, Kansas, and wrote his book. But Siringo wasn't at all the sedentary type, and he soon joined the Pinkerton National Detective Agency. He spent twenty years with Pinkerton's, riding in pursuit of Butch Cassidy and members of the Hole in the Wall Gang, providing crucial testimony in the murder trials of the union leaders who were behind the

1892 riots and bombings in Idaho, and generally leading a life of high adventure that would enthrall the readers of later books such as *The Cowboy Detective* (1912), *Lone Star Cowboy* (1919), *A History of Billy the Kid* (1920), and *Riata and Spurs* (1927).

Charley Siringo died at the age of seventy-three in 1928, one of the last survivors of the trail-driving era. Historian J. Frank Dobie has said of him, "No other cowboy ever talked about himself so much in print; few had as much to talk about."

Talking Us Through the Game

J OE GARAGIOLA WAS A solid enough baseball player to spend eight years in the major leagues, with the Cardinals, the Pirates, the Cubs, and the New York Giants—a career that came to an end after an arm injury sustained in a collision with Jackie Robinson. He wasn't a star, and had only a .257 lifetime batting average, but he was dependable.

In the world of broadcasting, however, it was different. Garagiola is still very dependable, but he's also a star, and people have been welcoming him into their homes via radio and television for thirty-seven years.

Born in St. Louis on February 12, 1926, the son of an immigrant bricklayer, Garagiola was a natural for the broadcasting booth. While still a player, his wit was famous around the clubhouses and on the off-season banquet circuit. He's been broadcasting sports events, chiefly baseball, since 1955. Whether it was NBC's *Game of the Week*, all-star games, playoffs, or World Series games, Garagiola could be counted on not only to get across what was happening on the field, but to leaven the account with amusing stories and sometimes pointed wit. "They sign for bonuses," he once said about the new players coming up. "If you know where home plate is—

fifty thousand dollars. If you know where first base is—twenty-five thousand dollars."

But his broadcasting career has covered a lot more ground than baseball. He's been the host of several game shows, from *To Tell the Truth* to *Strike It Rich*. He was a regular on the *Today Show* from 1969 to 1973, and was brought back in 1990 to help calm things down after a period of backstage feuding.

Joe Garagiola's wit can be sharp at times, but his easygoing nature and big smile can always be counted on to keep things from getting too heavy. He has always been one of those special television personalities who seems to be someone we know and are always glad to spend some time with.

Baseball Wits

ONNECT EACH OF THE following quotations with the correct speaker in the right-hand column.

a. My first year and a half there, they were serving a lot of Alpo in the clubhouse.	1. Yogi Berra
b. All last year we tried to teach him English, and the only word he learned was *million.*	2. Joe Garagiola
c. It gets late early out there.	3. Joe DiMaggio
d. Never trust a baseman who's limping. Comes a base hit and you'll think he just got back from Lourdes.	4. Ron Luciano
e. There is always some kid who may be seeing me for the first time or the last time. I owe him my best.	5. Tommy Lasorda
f. Carrots might be good for my eyes, but they won't straighten out the curveball.	6. Tony La Russa
g. He's a sinkerball pitcher, and like all things that sink, they tend to get wet once in a while.	7. Carl Furillo

The answers are as follows:

(a–6) Tony La Russa was not happy with the quality of his players when he began managing the Chicago White Sox in the mid-1980s.

(b–5) Dodger manager Tommy Lasorda was not at all happy about pitcher Fernando Valenzuel's 1982 salary hold-out.

(c–1) Yogi Berra gave one of his most concise explanations concerning the problem with afternoon shadows in the outfield at Yankee Stadium.

(d–2) Joe Garagiola could always be counted on for colorful commentary on baseball games.

(e–3) No one in baseball ever set higher standards for himself than Joe DiMaggio.

(f–7) Although Dodger great Carl Furillo won the National League batting championship in 1953 with a .344 average, he always claimed to have trouble with curveballs.

(g–4) Former umpire Ron Luciano was convinced pitcher Steve Rogers doctored the ball.

Tough, Elegant, and Whimsical

●•●•━•●•●•●•━•●•●•━•●•●•━•●•●•━•●

SOME INDIVIDUALS SEEM TO be composed of such contra-dictory elements that it becomes difficult to see them as whole people. Take Paul Gallico, the son of a father who emigrated to the United States from the Lombardy area of Italy, and a mother who came from Vienna.

Born July 26, 1897 in New York City, Gallico fought in the First World War as a gunner's mate. He then became a sportswriter for the *New York Daily News* and eventually an assistant managing editor of the paper. He won an Oscar nomination in 1942 for his original story about baseball legend, Lou Gehrig, *The Pride of the Yankees*, and then went off to fight with the U.S. Expeditionary Forces in World War II Europe.

But Paul Gallico had another side to him that brought him even greater acclaim, and a devoted readership that put one after another of his books on the best-seller lists. Many of these books were fables about animals, some haunting, others comic. There was *The Snow Goose* (1940), *The Small Miracle* (1952), *Thomasina* (1957), and *Scruffy* (1962). There was also a whole series of novels about a lower-class English widow, the plucky "Mrs. 'Arris," whose amusing adventures engaged readers for a dozen years from the mid-1950s on.

And there was still another personal side to Gallico: He was a sportsman whose own favorite exercise was fencing; a debonair man of the world totally at home in elite social circles (his fourth and last wife was a baroness); a man who spent many years living in London, where he was a member of many of the best clubs—this, too, was Paul Gallico.

While not the kind of writer who will be studied in literature classes, Gallico gave great pleasure to enormous numbers of readers around the world, and had a wonderful time on his own. Few of us can aspire to more than that.

The very beautiful and very talented Anne Bancroft shortly after filming The Miracle Worker. *Her role as Anne Sullivan, Helen Keller's tireless teacher, won acclaim both on Broadway and in movie theaters across the country but stands as only one of her many theatrical achievements.* ARCHIVE PHOTOS

Star from the Bronx

●▬●▬●▬●▬●▬●▬●▬●▬●▬●▬●▬●▬●▬●▬●▬●

BORN ON SEPTEMBER 17, 1931 IN the Bronx, New York, Anna Maria Louisa Italiano began acting on television in her late teens under the name Anne Amarno. By the time she was twenty-one, she had been signed to a contract by Twentieth Century Fox. Now known as Anne Bancroft, she made her feature-film debut in 1952 in *Don't Bother to Knock*, starring Richard Widmark and Marilyn Monroe, who played a psychotic baby-sitter, her best role up to that time.

Few of the other movies Bancroft made over the next five years were as good as her first, and many were even below the B-picture rank. Seeing Hollywood as a dead end, she returned to New York. Within a year, as the result of a legendary audition, she had snatched the female lead in the two-character comedy *Two for the Seesaw* right out of the hands of much better-known actresses. Her role opposite Henry Fonda brought her the Tony Award as Best Featured Actress and led to an even greater success and another Tony Award, this time as Best Actress in *The Miracle Worker*.

She'd left Hollywood as a minor B-movie actress, but returned in 1962 as a star to repeat her role as Annie Sullivan, Helen Keller's devoted teacher, in *The Miracle Worker*, for which she walked off with the Best Actress Oscar. She has been a star ever since, garnering four more Best Actress nominations for *The Pumpkin Eater* (1964), *The Graduate* (1967), *The Turning Point* (1977), and *Agnes of God* (1985).

> **Q.** For what movie did Anne Bancroft win the British Film Academy Award but not the Oscar?
>
> **A.** *The Pumpkin Eater,* a British film in which she costarred with Peter Finch and James Mason. She won both awards for *The Miracle Worker.*

Throughout her career, Anne Bancroft has proved herself equally adept at serious and comedic roles, moving easily from the emotional intensity of *The Elephant Man* (1980) to the broad farce of *To Be or Not to Be* (1983). Both of these movies were produced by her husband since 1964, Mel Brooks, and he also directed and costarred in the latter.

The Art of Never
Giving Up

•▬•▬•▬•▬•▬•▬•▬•▬•▬•▬•▬•▬•▬•▬•▬•

HOW DO YOU GET to be very famous and very rich in a
single year when you're practically a nobody? One way
is to write a screenplay that a lot of people want to produce,
and then refuse to sell it unless you are allowed to star in the
movie.

That's how Sylvester Stallone did it in 1976. An actor with
only minor roles in half a dozen movies (starting with Woody
Allen's *Bananas* in 1971), he finally negotiated a deal that
gave him only a small payment for the screenplay, with a
percentage of the profits. Rocky cost only $1.5 million to make
and took in $55.9 million at the box office. Audiences loved
it, critics liked it, and the Academy of Motion Picture Arts
and Sciences rewarded it with nine Oscar nominations, including two for Stallone himself, both as Best Actor and screenwriter. Although he didn't win a personal Oscar, the movie
was named Best Picture, John G. Avildsen picked up the Best
Director award, and it also won for best film editing.

Sylvester Stallone was born July 6, 1946, and grew up in
the tough Hell's Kitchen area on the West Side of New York
City. He first started acting at a boys' school outside Philadelphia, where his family had moved. He got more serious
about it while attending the American College in Geneva,

Switzerland, and as a drama major at the University of Miami, which he dropped out of thinking he was ready for the big time in New York. He may have been ready, but New York wasn't. He was reduced to taking a role in a semipornographic movie (which was promptly renamed *The Italian Stallion* after his success), but his only respectable credit was the bit part as a subway thug in *Bananas*. He didn't get another movie job until he was cast as one of several leads in 1974's low-budget *The Lords of Flatbush*, which was liked by some of the critics but brought Stallone only minor roles in five movies over the next year and a half. But Stallone had been writing film scripts for years; none of them sold, but he had learned his craft well, and *Rocky* suddenly got a lot of people interested in "Sly" Stallone.

Stallone followed up *Rocky* with two flops in a row. *F.I.S.T.*, which he cowrote and starred in was directed by Norman Jewison, and although the movie has its admirers, Stallone got knocked at the time for "one-dimensional" acting. The backlash really set in with *Paradise Alley*, also released in 1978, which Sly not only wrote and starred in but also directed. The critics bashed him with everything they had, taking particular note of the fact that he even sang the title song.

Stallone came right back with *Rocky II* in 1979, again writing, starring, and directing—but not singing. It was a box-office hit—all five of the "Rocky" films have done well at the box office, although they vary a lot in quality. Stallone was also capable of generating lines outside movie theaters with his *Rambo* movies, released in 1982, 1986, and 1988, but the third *Rambo III* was at the time the most expensive movie ever made, at some sixty million dollars, and didn't turn a profit.

For a superstar, Stallone has had a lot of flops, movies like *Rhinestone* (1984), *Over the Top* (1989), and *Oscar* (1991).

The jury is still out on his career as a whole, but he has always shown a willingness to try something different, and like Rocky himself, keeps bouncing back. There are few people in Hollywood with more sheer gumption, to use an old-fashioned word that fits Stallone like a boxing mitt, and as a triple-threat artist—actor, writer, and director—audiences and critics alike seem to expect him to wow them again with that next movie, or at least the one after that.

The Literature of Sweat

●~●~●~●~●~●~●~●~●~●~●~●~●~●~●~●~●~●

THE SON OF AN immigrant bricklayer, Geremio, and his wife, Annunziata, Pietro di Donato was born on April 3, 1911, in West Hoboken, New Jersey. He himself became a bricklayer, helping to support a large family after his father's accidental death.

A self-taught writer, he made his mark with the autobiographical novel *Christ in Concrete*, a Book-of-the-Month Club selection and best-seller in 1939. He went on to write additional novels, short stories, plays, and biographies of Mother Cabrini and Hawthorne, but it is *Christ in Concrete* that remains his most lasting contribution to American literature.

Few if any other novels have conveyed the hard realities of the immigrant Italian laborer's life with such vividness and passion. Critics noted that he wrote about his characters with "the deep human understanding of a prophet," and that his style "throbs with reality, with the feel of brick and mortar, the smells of labor, the tang of sour wine and olive oil and red peppers."

Reissued in 1975, *Christ in Concrete* remains required reading for any student of the immigrant experience in America.

"My Hero"

Q. Angelo Siciliano was born on a farm in Acri, Italy, in 1894. His family came to the United States and settled in Brooklyn, New York, in 1904. In the mid-1920s he changed his name and by the mid-1930s, had become known in practically every household in America. From the following clues can you figure out the name by which he became famous?

Clue #1: As a child, Angelo was often sick, and grew up to be a very skinny and underweight teenager, who was beaten up by bullies more than once.

Clue #2: Trying to improve his physical condition, he met with little success until he developed a system of his own.

Clue #3: A janitor in Coney Island, he first came to public attention by winning a national contest in 1922.

Clue #4: When he devised his new name, he took a very American first name, and a last name suggested by a neo-classical statue at a local bank.

Clue #5: By the mid-1930s, ads for the program he had created could be found in dozens of comic books, magazines, and newspapers.

Clue #6: The ads consisted of a series of drawings of events taking place on a beach, and the key to his program was what he called "dynamic tension."

A. The name Angelo Siciliano adopted was Charles Atlas. The one-time "97-pound weakling" used his own method of muscle-building to win that 1922 contest as the "World's Most Perfectly Developed Man." His advertising campaign, which was never changed, showed a skinny kid getting sand kicked in his face by a hefty bully who goes off with the skinny kid's girl. After taking a Charles Atlas course, the now magnificently muscled young man takes his girl back from the bully with a single punch. This brilliantly simple ad fueled a correspondence-course business that made Charles Atlas a wealthy man and an icon of American popular culture right up to his death at the age of seventy-eight in 1972.

Running the Game

●━●━●━●━●━●━●━●━●━●━●━●━●━●━●━●━●

THERE WERE A LOT of grumbles and snickers when Pete
Rozelle was named commissioner of the National Football
League in 1960. To begin with, he was very young, just thirty-
four, and he had never played football—tennis was his game.
The "child commissioner," some said, while others referred
to him as a "net jumper." The degree to which they were
wrong is indicated by the fact that within only a few years,
critics on the sidelines were calling him "ruthless" and "obsessed with money," while those who played and coached the
game were howling about his tough rules guarding against any
possibility of scandal.

Born on March 1, 1926, in South Gate, California, Rozelle
went to the University of San Francisco, where he became
athletic news director for the college while still working toward
his B.A. On graduation, he became assistant athletic director,
and only two years later was hired by the Los Angeles Rams
as their public relations director. From 1955 to 1957 he was
a partner in a private public relations firm and then was tapped
to become general manager of the Rams at the age of thirty-
one, the youngest manager by far in football.

Three years later, he was commissioner, and proved his
mettle with a bang in his first year by suspending Green Bay

Packer star Paul Hornung for gambling (even though it wasn't on Packer games). He would later force New York Jets legend Joe Namath to sell his interest in a New York restaurant where too many bookies hung out. But it was his genius for negotiating lucrative financial deals for professional football, out-maneuvering the titans of television at every turn, that was the special mark of his years as commissioner. He even managed to persuade Congress to exempt pro football from the antitrust laws, thus enabling the highly lucrative merger of the NFL and the AFL to take place, and the creation of the Super Bowl.

By the time he retired in 1989, after twenty-nine years at the helm, Rozelle had turned pro football into a money-making machine, while at the same time keeping it free of the ever-present threat of a gambling scandal. At the end of his tenure he also began to take tough steps to stem the rising amount of drug use clouding all professional sports. Pete Rozelle had proved himself to be a lot more than a mere tennis player.

Rozelle was succeeded as NFL commissioner by another Italian American, Paul John Tagliabue, a prominent Washington lawyer who was born on November 24, 1940, in Jersey City, New Jersey. Pete Rozelle had proved that you didn't need someone who had played football to be its commissioner, and in the process, he had created a business empire that then did need a lawyer at the top.

That Crazy Kid

●■●■●■●■●■●■●■●■●■●■●■●■●■●

> **Q.** In the mid-1930s, the game of basketball was revolution-
> ized by Angelo Enrico Luisetti, known as Hank. Did he ever
> play the game professionally?
>
> **A.** No.

IN HIGH SCHOOL IN San Francisco, this son of a chef who had
emigrated from Italy, was disdained by the basketball coach,
who took exception to a one-handed shot young Hank had
developed. That wasn't the way you played basketball, the
coach insisted. None of the speed, dazzling moves, and rapid-
fire passing we associate with the game today existed then.
Basketball was a slow, almost lumbering game—and everybody
used a two-handed shot.

But Hank Luisetti got lucky. He was admitted to Stanford
University, and the basketball coach there was astonished at
the freshman's ability. In only eighteen games, Hank scored
305 points. Those were unheard-of numbers, and the Stanford
team had an undefeated season. The next year he added an
additional 111 points to that total. He became the first college
player to score 50 points in a game, and he was twice selected
as an All-American.

The high point, as Mac Davis reports in *The Giant Book of Sports*, came in 1938, when the Stanford team traveled east to play Long Island University, the top team in the country. Long Island had won forty-three games in a row, but Hank Luisetti saw to it that the streak was ended. More important for the game of basketball as a whole, the game that winter night was attended by many of the top coaches in America, and what they saw Hank Luisetti do on the court caused them to completely rethink how the game was played. The one-handed shot of the young man many people had called "that crazy kid" would become part of the game forever.

Although the NBA would not be created until 1946, there were professional basketball teams in the mid-1930s, mostly on the East Coast. But Hank Luisetti never got to play with any of them. In his senior year at Stanford, he contracted spinal meningitis and it was all doctors could do to save his life. He would never play basketball again, but he had changed the way it was played—and he had done it singlehandedly, in more ways than one.

Early Retirement?

•◦•◦••◦••◦•◦••◦•◦•◦••◦•◦••◦••◦•◦••◦•

A<small>T THE AGE OF</small> twenty-eight, Anna Maria Alberghetti retired. And why not; she had been a professional singer
and actress for twenty-two years by then.

The daughter of musicians, she was born in Pesaro, Italy,
on May 15, 1936, and made her singing debut at the age of
six. At twelve she made a concert tour of Europe. She first
came to America when she was fourteen, making her debut
at Carnegie Hall, the citadel of American concert stages.

In 1951, Alberghetti made her first movie, a film version
of Gian-Carlo Menotti's *The Medium*. In the course of the
following decade, she made many more movies, including
Here Comes the Groom (1951), *The Last Command* (1955),
and *Cinderfella* (1960), but Hollywood never really used her
talents fully, and her great popularity was as much based on
her records and concert appearances as it was on her films.
On television, she was much in demand as a guest star, of
Bob Hope, Eddie Fisher, and Red Skelton, among others.

Then in 1962 she was finally given an opportunity to show
her true range as the star of the Broadway musical *Carnival*,
based on the beloved movie *Lili*, but with an entirely new
score and a magical staging by Gower Champion. Taking on
a role so identified with Leslie Caron didn't faze her for a

moment. With her dark hair, translucent skin, and big, liquid eyes, she luminously made the role her own. She was rewarded with a Tony for Best Actress in a Musical (in a rare tie, with Diahann Carroll for her role in Richard Rodgers's musical *No Strings*). With a triumph commensurate with her talents, she retired, Tony in hand, to California.

A Mellow Man

●❀●❀●❀●❀●❀●❀●❀●❀●❀●❀●❀●❀●

IT ISN'T "I LEFT My Heart in San Francisco" that is Tony
Bennett's favorite song, even though it has become his sig-
nature tune and won him Grammy Awards for Record of the
Year and Best Male Solo in 1962. The song he holds the
fondest place for in his heart is "Boulevard of Broken Dreams,"
which was his first major hit and established him as a popular
singer. It's an ironic choice, because while dozens of other
singers have hit the top of the charts and then faded from view
after only a few years, Tony Bennett has sung his way through
more than four decades of success with hardly a stumble along
the road.

Anthony Dominick Benedetto, the son of a tailor, was born
August 3, 1926, and grew up during the Depression in Astoria,
Queens, a section of New York City. Despite financial hard-
ships, his was a close-knit and loving family—something Bennett credits for his personal stability over his long career.

Although he had been singing since he was a teenager,
Bennett really began his career after serving in the armed forces
in World War II. At first, it was small clubs all over the map,
but then he began to be noticed by other performers. Pearl
Bailey and Bob Hope were among the first to champion him—
as well as teach him about how to sell himself to an audience.

The remarkable voice was always there, but the style of his performance, the relaxed and smiling presence he exudes, developed over time.

Soon other stars were throwing bouquets at him, with both Frank Sinatra and Bing Crosby saying he had the best voice around. But audiences didn't really need to be told that, and they went right on packing his concerts and club dates, despite the fact that Bennett refused to move in the direction of rock 'n' roll. It just wasn't him, and he insisted on introducing songs with equal emphasis on words and music.

Bennett came out of Astoria, Queens, and ended up singing at the Waldorf-Astoria, not to mention Carnegie Hall and the Royal Albert Hall in London. He's sung in Las Vegas year after year, and on all the television variety shows and talk shows that have come and gone, including Johnny Carson's very first *Tonight Show* (as well as one of Johnny's last).

Bennett is also an accomplished watercolorist and oil painter, whose work has been shown in many galleries—another artistic endeavor that goes back to his teens. But for all his talents, it is perhaps something more indefinable that has kept him a favorite through the decades: Tony Bennett is somehow just a nice guy to have around.

Music in Your Dreams

●▸●▸●▸●▸●▸●▸●▸●▸●▸●▸●▸●▸●●

O N MAY 22, 1992, ONE OF the best-known—maybe *the* best-known—themes ever written for television was retired. Along with the retirement of Johnny Carson, the theme for *The Tonight Show*, dashed off years earlier by the then-twenty-one-year-old singer/composer Paul Anka, made way for a new theme by Branford Marsalis. Although Johnny Carson was known before *Tonight* for a successful quiz show he had hosted, Anka was undoubtedly more famous at the time. He had become a teenage pop idol at the age of fourteen, in 1956, and was already the veteran of world-tour concert performances.

Born on July 30, 1941, in Ottawa, Canada, Anka settled permanently in the United States in 1959. He was sensationally popular when he was young, but managed to make the transition gracefully from arenas full of screaming teenagers to posh New York nightclubs, and later to Las Vegas hotel showrooms. At the height of his career, he played many famous halls, including the Palladium in London and the Olympia in Paris.

Married since 1963 to the former Anne de Zognheb, Anka, his wife, and five children, have managed to lead a life virtually free of tabloid headlines. He attributes much of the steadiness of his life to his family, but also exhibits a relaxed and good-natured personality unusual among people who have become superstars when still in their teens.

Perhaps one of the secrets of Paul Anka's equanimity is that he has a second string to his bow as a composer. Not only has he written numerous hits for himself, going all the way back to the 1957 jukebox favorite "Diana," but has also been sought out by other top singers to compose songs especially for them. Both Frank Sinatra's anthem, "My Way," and the Tom Jones hit "She's a Lady," are Paul Anka songs. But it is probably the theme for *The Tonight Show* that people hear most often in their dreams.

Discovering What We Are Made Of

•▬•▬•▬•▬•▬•▬•▬•▬•▬•▬•▬•▬•▬•▬•▬•

"Bᴀᴄ-ᴛᴇ̄'-ʀɪ-ᴏ̄-ᴘʜᴀ̄ɢᴇ, ɴ. [ʙᴀᴄᴛᴇʀɪᴏ- ᴀɴᴅ -phage] a micro-scopic agent that destroys disease-producing bacteria in a living organism."

OK, so these agents don't sound like much, but back in the late 1940s, a lot of researchers in the fields of medicine and physiology started to get very interested in them, both in Europe and the United States. In Italy, they intrigued a young man named Salvador Luria, who had gained his M.D., with highest honors, at the University of Turin in 1935. In 1940, Luria fled Fascist Italy for the United States, where he spent two years as a research assistant at Columbia University. Then a Guggenheim grant took him to Vanderbilt University in Nashville, Tennessee.

At Vanderbilt, Luria encountered two other researchers who were also working on bacteriophage viruses: Max Delbrück, who had come to America from Germany in 1937, and the American-born Alfred D. Hershey. By irradiating the viruses and studying them through the electron microscope that was just coming into use, they were able to observe that the viruses mutated from one generation to the next, a fact that became one of the cornerstones of molecular biology.

The 1953 identification of the structure of DNA, the

building-block of genetics, by James D. Watson and Francis H. C. Crick, flowed from the work of Luria, Delbrück, and Hershey. The identification of DNA was of such monumental importance that it brought Watson and Crick the Nobel Prize in 1962 for Medicine. As often happens in the sciences, the underlying work of Luria and his two colleagues was not recognized by the Nobel committee until 1969. But the Nobel Prize given them made their role abundantly clear, citing them for having "set the solid foundation on which modern molecular biology rests."

Salvador Luria was immensely respected as a biologist (his *General Virology* became the standard text in the field), but he was always a man of social conscience as well. Like his fellow Italian-American Nobel winner, nuclear physicist Enrico Fermi, he warned against the consequences of the misuse of his discoveries. He was also a champion of the poor in America, whom he felt were being neglected because of misplaced priorities, especially in the area of defense. Much of his share of the Nobel Prize money was donated to groups protesting the war in Vietnam.

Like so many great scientists, Luria, who died in 1991 at the age of seventy-nine, dedicated his life to expanding man's knowledge of our universe, while at the same time advocating that people must come first.

Big Talents in a
Small Package

I F YOU'RE A VERY short man, and kind of funny-looking, and none too slim, can you get to be a movie star? It's traditionally very unlikely, unless you have the talent of a Danny DeVito. Just how unlikely DeVito's rise to fame as both actor and director is can be measured by his first post–high-school educational credit: the Wilfred Academy of Hair and Beauty Culture. But he soon moved on to the American Academy of Dramatic Arts in New York.

Born November 17, 1944, in Neptune, New Jersey, DeVito went through several years of stage and minor movie roles before making his first major impression on audiences in 1975's Oscar-winning Best Picture *One Flew Over the Cuckoo's Nest*. His next few movies were little seen and didn't further his career, but he had a great success on television in the sitcom *Taxi* (1978 to 1982). He had effective but minor roles in 1983's Best Picture *Terms of Endearment* and 1984's *Johnny Dangerously*, but his Hollywood career began to take off later in 1984, when he was cast as the irascible foil to Michael Douglas (who had produced *Cuckoo*) in the big hit *Romancing the Stone*, and its 1985 sequel, *The Jewel of the Nile*.

His comic range became even more apparent as Bette Midler's husband, thrilled at her kidnapping, in 1986's *Ruthless*

People. He was then given the chance to direct himself in the hilarious spin on Hitchcock's classic *Strangers on a Train*, 1987's *Throw Momma from the Train*, which elevated Billy Crystal to real stardom and brought a Best Supporting Actress nomination to "Momma," Anne Ramsey.

For other directors, a more serious role in *Tin Men* (1987), and a charming turn as Arnold Schwarzenegger's (nonidentical) twin in *Twins*, capped by a scenery-chewing tour de force as the Penguin in 1992's blockbuster *Batman Returns*, have solidified his status as one of America's favorite actors. As a director, his ability to turn the chancy dark-hued *The War of the Roses* (1989) into a commercial hit gave him the chance to produce, direct, and star in—together with Jack Nicholson—*Hoffa*.

Married to award-winning *Cheers* actress Rhea Perlman, with four children, DeVito has bucked Hollywood tradition and come out head and shoulders above the rest.

"The Great Lover"

•‑•‑•‑•‑•‑•‑•‑•‑•‑•‑•‑•‑•‑•‑•‑•‑•‑•‑•

HIS FIRST WIFE LOCKED him out of the bedroom on his wedding night, and the marriage was never consummated.

He let his second wife dictate his career, which she almost destroyed with disastrous choices.

Many men found him embarrassing to watch.

When he died at thirty-one, some women committed suicide in a frenzy of grief.

Who was he? Rodolfo Alfonzo Raffaelo Pierre Filibert Guglielmi di Valentina d'Antonguolla, Hollywood's first male legend.

Rudolph Valentino was in many ways an unlikely superstar, and never a very happy one. Born in Castellaneta, Italy, he was the son of a veterinarian for the army cavalry. His father's death when he was twelve left him a rather directionless young man, who made various half-hearted stabs at finding a career before emigrating to New York City in 1913 at the age of eighteen. There he worked as a gardener—he had had some agricultural training in Italy—and as a waiter. But he had one true gift: He was a startlingly fluid and sensual exhibition dancer, and was soon making a living in New York clubs.

By means of a cross-country tour as a dancer in a musical, he ended up on the West Coast and decided to try his luck with the

Rudolph Valentino focusing his classic stare in the 1924 film
The Sainted Devil. *His look made him the most adored man
of his time and the greatest romantic legend ever.*
ARCHIVE PHOTOS

fledgling movie industry in Los Angeles. For more than three years, from 1917 on, he landed secondary (or minor) roles in a number of negligible movies. Appropriately enough, it was a woman who saw the potential star in him. Her name was June Mathis. She had been a screenwriter since 1917, and was respected in Hollywood in a way that is unusual even now, seventy-five years later. The screenwriter for the first film of Blasco Ibáñez's famous novel *The Four Horsemen of the Apocalypse*, in 1921, she persuaded the director Rex Ingram that Valentino was right for the leading role. The movie—brilliantly photographed—was in many ways a very grim antiwar movie (striking a chord with the public in the aftermath of the horrors of World War I), but it contained a sequence early in the film in which Valentino danced the tango with a power and eroticism that was new to the screen. The epic became one of the most successful movies of the decade, and Valentino's stardom was assured.

Valentino quickly built on his success with *The Sheik* (1921) and a version of the earlier Ibáñez novel about bullfighting, *Blood and Sand* (1922). To the fury of many American men from English or northern-European ancestries, the Latin Valentino was suddenly seen as a "great lover." Women went absolutely wild over him while their husbands and boyfriends fumed. But then he married his second wife, Natasha Rambova, a sometime actress and scenic designer, who almost turned him into a joke.

Q. What was Natasha Rambova's real name?

   a. Natalie Ramsey
   b. Winifred Shaunessy
   c. Rosa Sacchi

A. The answer is b.

Rambova began using her great influence over Valentino not only in terms of choosing his scripts, but also in regard to his costuming and makeup. The first of the movies she talked him into doing, *The Young Rajah*, released in 1922 after the triumph of *Blood and Sand*, was such a catastrophe that Valentino did not make another movie for more than a year. In 1924 came *Monsieur Bocaire*, which did all right at the box office, but it was followed in the same year by A *Sainted Devil* and in 1925, *Cobra*, neither of which was popular. The trouble was not just bad or inappropriate scripts, it was the way Rambova was making her husband look. He was so prettified that he began to be referred to as the "pink powderpuff" and the "painted pansy." The many male moviegoers who had always disliked him were getting their revenge, and women were becoming disenchanted as well.

Valentino's studio, Paramount, was also fed up, and the actor moved over to United Artists in 1925, a company whose executives had the good sense to demand a contract that forbade the participation of the dreaded Rambova in any way. Valentino tried to make up for this "betrayal" by putting up his own money to back *What Price Beauty?* which Rambova both produced and directed. The critics hooted, the public stayed away, and Rambova left Valentino.

But with Rambova's influence lifted, Valentino went on to make two of his biggest hits, *The Eagle* in 1925, and *Son of the Sheik* in 1926. These would be his last films. On August 23, 1926, he died in New York, the victim of a perforated ulcer that he had ignored. News of his death at the age of thirty-one caused what can only be called pandemonium in New York, where the scene outside Campbell's Funeral Home on the Upper West Side required the intervention of riot police. Pola Negri, the exotic silent star from Russia who had been having an affair with Valentino, made a cross-country tour dramatizing her grief for thousands of nearly hysterical women.

Valentino fan clubs continued to flourish for decades. Like Marilyn Monroe, James Dean, and Elvis, Valentino passed into the realm of legend.

The Diva from Connecticut

◆●◆●◆●◆●◆●◆●◆●◆●◆●◆●◆●◆●◆●◆●◆●◆

NOVEMBER 15, 1918, WAS A HISTORIC night at the Metropolitan Opera in New York City. It marked the company's first performance of Verdi's *La Forza del Destino*, originally composed in 1862, but later considerably revised. The legendary tenor Enrico Caruso starred as the protagonist, Don Alvaro, and the chance to see Caruso in a new role was in itself sufficient to cause great anticipation. There were also three singers making their debuts that night, but the talk, both before and after the performance, centered on a twenty-one-year-old soprano from Meriden, Connecticut, who had taken the name Rosa Ponselle. She was scheduled to sing the leading female role of Leonora, daughter of Don Alvaro.

Until very recently, Rosa Ponselle had been performing with her sister Carmella, a mezzo-soprano, as the Ponzillo Sisters— in vaudeville! Caruso himself had encouraged her to make the move to grand opera. Had he taken leave of his senses? Would his protégée prove to be worthy of the Metropolitan, let alone the greatest tenor ever known?

Rosa Ponzillo made the leap to opera diva in one night, even though her new name was misspelled in the program as Poncelle. For the following nineteen years she was one of the Metropolitan Opera's greatest draws, mastering an exceptionally broad range of roles from Carmen to Aida to Donna Anna in *Don Giovanni*. In the title role of Ponchielli's *La Gioconda*, she was such a success that this minor opera remained in the repertory for eleven consecutive seasons. She was regarded as the greatest Norma of her time, and could even turn Gasparo Spontini's *La Vestale*, which had not been heard in New York for nearly a century, into a personal triumph in 1925.

Rosa Ponselle moved on to conquer London, singing at Covent Garden in several of her most famous roles from 1929 to 1931. She continued singing at the Metropolitan until 1937, then became a sought-after teacher, and also directed opera in Baltimore for many years. The diva from Meriden, Connecticut, died at the age of eighty-four in 1981.

What a Voice!

•▰•▰•▰•▰•▰•▰•▰•▰•▰•▰•▰•▰•▰•▰•

MARIO LANZA WAS BORN Alfredo Cocozza in Philadelphia
on January 31, 1921, and died in Rome on October 7,
1959, his health broken by binge eating alternating with star-
vation diets and a debilitating alcohol problem. His story is
tragic—he had so much to offer and never quite lived up to
his promise. But he deserves inclusion here because during
his short life he brought immeasurable pleasure to millions of
people.

His road to fame began in 1942, when he was brought
backstage to meet the great conductor Serge Koussevitzky, who
was appearing at the Philadelphia Academy of Music with his
Boston Symphony Orchestra. It was the afternoon before the
performance, and the conductor, who was busy and simply
doing a favor, had no real expectations of making any kind of
discovery. But all he had to hear was Lanza (who had taken
his mother's name as a performer) singing a warm-up aria in
another room. He was immediately asked to spend the summer
at the Berkshire Music Festival at Tanglewood, which Koussevitzky had founded in 1934, and offered a scholarship. Lanza
sang in a concert at Tanglewood on August 7 that summer
and was given a rave review by Noel Strauss of *The New York
Times*. He was quickly signed by Columbia Artists, but then

found himself inducted into the army. His voice got him an assignment with a touring GI show and then landed him in the all-serviceman Broadway production, *Winged Victory.*

After the war, he was taken on by a New York manager named Sam Weiler, who set up lessons with the great opera teacher Enrico Rosati. Rosati never felt that Lanza worked hard enough, and while he did manage to teach the young singer a good deal, he also contributed to Lanza's deep sense of insecurity.

From July 1947 to May 1948, Lanza toured across the country with an old army pal, George London, who was destined to become a great star of the Metropolitan, and the soprano Frances Yeend. They often played to huge crowds, including a hundred twenty thousand people in Chicago's Grant Park, and everywhere people were simply bowled over by Lanza's voice. But London and Yeend had a difficult time with him—Lanza suffered from dreadful stage fright, and often drank in order to get himself out on stage.

A concert at Hollywood Bowl eventually led to a movie contract with MGM. Louis B. Mayer was dubious about the appeal of the somewhat beefy young man, but producer Joe Pasternak championed him. On a tour leading up to the release of his first movie, *That Midnight Kiss* (1949), Lanza's stage fright caused him to cancel fifteen out of twenty-seven appearances. But the movie was a hit and so was his next venture, *The Toast of New Orleans* (1950), both costarring Kathryn Grayson. Lanza wanted to do a movie about Enrico Caruso, but the MGM money men, whom Mayer was by now in thrall to, were against it. Mayer fought for the project and *The Great Caruso* (1951) turned out to be a huge hit, selling out Radio City Music Hall for ten weeks. The recording earned Lanza an incredible five million dollars. He went on another concert tour, often earning up to six thousand dollars per performance, the highest fees paid up to that time. But in order to get through it, Lanza was drinking more and more.

He made *Because You're Mine* in 1952 and then was supposed to do what seemed an excellent project, *The Student Prince*. But he had gotten so heavy that after several postponements, the studio replaced him with Edmund Purdom and had him lip sync to Lanza's voice in the 1954 film. Although there were three more films, including the respectable *Serenade* (1956), Lanza was now on a steep downward path. His health was deteriorating, his concert appearances were very chancy affairs, and he seemed to have less and less ability to get control of himself, although he tried again and again. Amazingly, his voice did not desert him. If he could get on stage in a reasonably sober state, he could still thrill audiences.

He was greatly mourned when he died at the age of thirty-eight. Although his life was a personal disaster, his records are still cherished, his movies show up regularly on television, and to hear him at his best somehow wipes away the tragedy for many people. There have been few voices as beautiful since the beginning of recorded sound.

A Hit at the Met

•━•━•━•━•━•━•━•━•━•━•━•━•━•━•━•━•

D ECEMBER 1991 SAW A RARE event take place at the Metropolitan Opera in New York: the premiere of a new
opera commissioned by the company, the first such occasion
in more than two decades. Even rarer, John Corigliano's *The
Ghosts of Versailles*, with a libretto by William Hoffman, was
an immediate hit with audiences, and extremely well received
by critics.

Born in New York City on February 16, 1938, Corigliano
graduated cum laude from Columbia University and embarked
immediately on a composing career. His compositions for orchestra began attracting attention when he was still in his mid-
twenties, including the Violin Sonata of 1963 and *The Cloisters
for Voice and Orchestra* in 1965. His concertos for various
instruments and orchestra, particularly the Concerto for Oboe
and Orchestra (1975) and the Concerto for Clarinet and Orchestra (1977), were played by many orchestras around the
world. His particular mix of avant-garde effects and neo-
Romanticism has proved a remarkably successful fusion to
which audiences have responded warmly. His Symphony No. 1,
an AIDS memorial that premiered in 1990, has often left
listeners in tears.

Still a relatively young man, and continuing to grow as a

composer, Corigliano is regarded as one of the brightest lights among American composers of the second half of the century, and his new works are eagerly anticipated. But in creating the first widely accepted new American opera to be mounted by the Metropolitan in many years, he has already attained remarkable heights.

The Sexy Prima
Donna

•◄•►◄•►◄•►◄•►◄•►◄•►◄•►◄•►◄•►◄•►◄•►◄•►◄•►◄•►►◄•►►►•

IN THE EARLY 1960s, A beautiful Italian-American woman
born in Wayne, Pennsylvania, on June 27, 1932, became
the prototype of a new kind of opera star: the jet-set diva.
Anna Moffo had a ravishing soprano voice, the body of a
movie star (she once even appeared nude in an Italian film),
great charm, and an ability to make headlines. She hop-
scotched back and forth across the Atlantic and all over Europe, appearing at every major opera house on the map. Being
home-grown and glamorous, she was a major attraction at the
Metropolitan Opera in New York, where she made her debut
as Violetta in *La Traviata* in 1959. She was also extremely
popular in Italy, not only because she had become truly fluent
in the language during a Fulbright grant year following her
graduation from Philadelphia's Curtis Institute, but also because she understood the rules of being a prima donna in
Italy: If she didn't get what she wanted, she could faint at the
drop of a handkerchief.

Moffo ran into some difficulties with her voice in mid-
career—the critics blamed her hectic international schedule—
but got back on track and continued to have great success
through the 1970s, making dozens of recordings, thrilling op-

era house audiences with her emotional performances, and developing a high-profile concert career as well. "It's very hard to get to the top," she once said, "and it's even harder to stay there once you've made it." Anna Moffo has done both, and loved every minute of it.

Not a Pretty Face

A HULKING FRAME, A face that could be evil, comic, even tender, but never handsome, and an almost nonexistent waistline would hardly seem to suggest the potential for movie stardom. But the beefy guy from Hamden, Connecticut, born Ermes Effron Borgnino on January 24, 1917, had more than enough talent to make the grade in Hollywood, where there has always been room for a few male stars who didn't fit the romantic mold.

Ernest Borgnine spent the first years of his adulthood in the United States Navy, a ten-year hitch that saw him rise to the rank of chief gunner's mate. Out of the navy and determined to become an actor, he attended the Randall School of Dramatic Arts in Hartford, Connecticut, made his professional debut at Virginia's famed Barter Theater, and was on Broadway within a year, playing the mental-home attendant in the long-running Mary Chase hit *Harvey*. After more Broadway roles he became one of the stalwarts of early television drama, appearing in dozens of the plays that were broadcast live during television's "Golden Age."

He made three 1951 movies, starting with *China Corsair*. Then it was back to television until he was tapped to play the brutal "Fatso" in 1953's much-honored *From Here to Eternity*.

A young Ernest Borgnine a few years after winning an Oscar for Best Actor ARCHIVE PHOTOS

He was by then typed as a villain, and was a memorable one in such movies as *Vera Cruz* and the Freudian Western, *Johnny Guitar*, both released in 1954. But in between villains, Borgnine went back to New York and starred as a gentle, lovelorn butcher in a television drama called *Marty*. Hollywood decided to make it into a movie, with additional scenes, and for once, the movie-town honchos had the sense to stick with the role's creator instead of looking for a bigger name. His touching performance earned him the 1955 Best Actor Oscar over three of Hollywood's greatest stars, Spencer Tracy (nominated for *Bad Day at Black Rock*), James Cagney (*Love Me or Leave Me*), and Frank Sinatra (*The Man with the Golden Arm*) as well as the electrifying newcomer, James Dean (*East of Eden*). It certainly did not hurt that in the same year Borgnine gave still another vivid performance as a loathsome bully in *Bad Day at Black Rock*. Hollywood has always had great respect for actors who are able to demonstrate that they have a wide range as performers.

Q. Which, if any, of the following awards did Ernest Borgnine also win for his portrayal of *Marty*?

  a. The Golden Globe
  b. The National Board of Review Best Actor Award
  c. The New York Film Critics Award

A. He won all three. In addition, the entire cast was given a special citation by the Cannes Film Festival Jury, which gave *Marty* its top prize, the *Palme D'Or*.

But, as is often the case in Hollywood, Borgnine's demonstration of versatility caused a slowdown in his career—producers suddenly couldn't decide what kind of role he should be playing. The always resourceful Borgnine took care of that by returning to television to star in the very popular series *McHale's Navy*, which ran from 1962 to 1966. The former gunner's mate was absolutely at home in this role that allowed him to be both gruff and likable.

During the late 1960s and early 1970s, Borgnine had some of the best roles of his Hollywood career in such huge hits as *The Dirty Dozen*, *The Wild Bunch*, and *The Poseidon Adventure*. Although his movies were not always hits, he has continued to work as a character actor on into the 1990s.

Ernest Borgnine did not turn to the acting profession until his late twenties, but in a nearly fifty-year career, he proved himself in every medium—stage, television, and movies—capturing the profession's most coveted awards and doing honor to himself and his calling.

Up from the Streets

"WHEN YOU'RE IN ROME, you talk Italian, when you're in Jerusalem, you talk Jewish, and when you live on the East Side, you talk tough, like everybody else talks tough, and you do the things they do."

"Doing the things they do," for the man born Rocco Barbella, on June 7, 1922, in lower Manhattan, brought a stint in reform school. But Rocco was a smart kid who figured out there was something else to do with his toughness: get into professional boxing. With a great punch and fast reflexes, he rose quickly through the middleweight division, became known as Rocky Graziano, and was champion from 1947 to 1948.

Retiring in 1952, Graziano moved over to show business (with Rocky in the ring, it had always been a show), including a stint as a regular on *The Martha Raye Show*. He wrote a best-selling autobiography about getting to the top the hard way, called *Somebody Up There Likes Me*. The book was made into a movie in 1956. Hollywood's surprising choice to play Graziano was the very handsome, and thoroughly un-Italian Paul Newman, but Newman won wide critical praise for a remarkably gritty performance (even Rocky liked it), and the movie remains one of the best boxing films ever made.

With his engaging smile and quick wit, Graziano survived the mean streets and a sport that destroyed many men to take his place as one of the best-liked and most-admired boxers of the past half-century.

Little Flower

●◖●◖●◖●◖●◖●◖●◖●◖●◖●◖●◖●◖●◖●◖●

THE YEAR 1959 WAS A terrific one for Broadway musicals.
Not only was Jackie Gleason strutting his stuff in *Take Me
Along*—the musical adaptation of Eugene O'Neill's *Ah, Wil-
derness!*—but Mary Martin was having one of her greatest
triumphs in *The Sound of Music*, and Ethel Merman was
tearing up the stage as Mamma Rose in *Gypsy*. *Gypsy* and
The Sound of Music have become summer-stock staples of the
American musical theater, but in 1959 there was still another
musical on Broadway—one that walked off with the Pulitzer
Prize for Drama, the New York Drama Critics' Circle Award,
and tied with *The Sound of Music* for the Tony Awards for
Best Musical, Best Book, and Best Score. It was called *Fiorello!*,
and it celebrated the life and times of Mayor Fiorello (Little
Flower) H. La Guardia, who served three terms, from 1934
to 1945, as the flamboyant leader of New York City. The
young Tom Bosley, still very much with us on television, won
the Best Featured Actor Tony for his portrayal of the Little
Flower.

The musical is seldom revived, perhaps because it is just
too New York for the rest of the country. But it may also be
because, sadly, La Guardia himself is little known by anyone
under fifty. That is a shame, as he was not only the best-loved

Among his many achievements, Fiorello La Guardia is known for his great use of radio to keep in touch with his constituency. Here he gives the people of New York City an accounting of his first six months as mayor. ARCHIVE PHOTOS

mayor New York ever had, known across the land, but also one of the most respected and important congressmen in the years preceding his mayoralty. He was one of the most original political thinkers of his time, and a major reformer who changed the way politics worked in New York, a city long under the grip of the corrupt bosses of the Tammany Hall Democratic machine.

The son of an Italian bandmaster and a mother from Trieste of Jewish background, Austrian citizenship, and Italian culture, La Guardia was born in Greenwich Village in New York on December 11, 1882. Yet this quintessential New Yorker grew up in Arizona, where his father was the U.S. Army bandmaster at the fort at Prescott. At the outbreak of the Spanish-American War in 1898, his father was transferred to Mobile, Alabama. The teenage Fiorello managed to talk his way into a job as a war correspondent for the *St. Louis Post-Dispatch*. His father was then transferred to Tampa, where he contracted malaria, and the family went to Trieste. Following his father's death, La Guardia wangled a post as a clerk at the American consulate in Budapest, and after three years there, was put in charge of a branch office at Fiume, from which Balkan immigrants usually sailed to the United States. When he returned to New York at the age of twenty-three, his experience in Fiume got him a job as a translator at Ellis Island.

By 1910, La Guardia had earned a law degree at New York University and set about trying to make a better life for the immigrants whose miserable lives he was so well acquainted with. Disgusted with the corruption of the Tammany Democrats, La Guardia became a Republican (although these days he would be called a "flaming liberal")—the sacrificial-lamb candidate for Congress in 1914. He astonished everyone by doing remarkably well, and two years later, won the seat. He was reelected, but was asked by Republican leaders to give up his seat and run for president of New York City's board of aldermen, with the promise that he would be the Republican candidate for mayor in 1921. He followed orders reluctantly and won. He would have been happier to be in Congress, but his spirits were renewed by his marriage to Thea Almerigotti. The Republicans then backed out on the agreement to run him for mayor. In what turned out to be the disastrous year of 1921, he was badly beaten in the Republican primary, and both his wife and their infant daughter Fiorella died of tuberculosis.

La Guardia was wild with grief, but pulled himself together, and in 1923 he was back in Congress, where he would remain until 1933. He proposed all kinds of new ideas that were condemned as radical or scorned as absurd. But later, during his three terms as mayor of New York, from 1934 to 1945, Congress adopted one after another of his "wild" proposals: the minimum wage, child-labor laws, the repeal of Prohibition, and government regulation of the stock market.

In 1929, La Guardia married his long-time secretary, Marie Fisher, with whom he would have a son and a daughter. In 1934, he would finally break the back of the Tammany machine and with Marie at his side would for three terms run New York City with a fairness, openness, and incorruptability it had never seen from City Hall in living memory.

Fiorello La Guardia died on September 21, 1947, of cancer. The little man with the high, almost falsetto, voice had seen his ideas become the law of the land in a new age that he had helped immeasurably to usher in.

A Congressman Worth
the Title

•~•~•~•~•~•~•~•~•~•~•~•~•~•~•

BORN IN PITTSFIELD, MASSACHUSETTS, in 1922, Silvio Ottó Conte worked as a machinist after his graduation from high school, but soon found himself in the South Pacific serving as Seabee during World War II. Military service gave him a postwar opportunity he would not otherwise have had—to attend college, thanks to the GI Bill of Rights. He went through Boston College and its law school with dispatch, graduating in 1949 and then winning his first election, to the Massachusetts State Senate, the same year. Over the next forty-two years, Conte gave a good name to that now-tarnished phrase "career politician."

An independent mind and fearless spirit took him along a highly distinctive political path. At the very outset, he changed his party registration from Democrat to Republican—for the simple reason that he had been refused a job as a census taker even though Democrats controlled such patronage in his neck of the woods. Yet, once he was elected to Congress as a representative from his hometown district in the election of 1958, he steadfastly voted as he believed right, although as time went by, that more and more often meant joining the Democrats rather than supporting his own party.

He always took care of his district, which included both

blue-collar workers and the numerous institutions of higher learning in the northwest corner of Massachusetts including Amherst, Williams, Hampshire, Springfield College, the University of Massachusetts, a host of community colleges, and the women's colleges Smith and Mount Holyoke. But he did not believe in throwing around federal money for the purposes of simply getting reelected rather then supporting projects of genuine worth, and many members of Congress were stung over the years by his diatribes about useless "pork-barrel" legislation.

What did he believe were worthwhile projects? In order to prevent the extinction of passenger rail service, he authored the legislation creating Amtrak in 1970. He cosponsored the first legislation to provide funds for AIDS research back in 1983—before most politicians even wanted to hear about the problem. Together with his good friend Thomas P. "Tip" O'Neill, former Speaker of the House, he wrote a bill to provide the poor with help in paying their heating bills during the oil-crunch of the 1970s. Such collaborations with the Democratic leadership did not endear him to the increasingly conservative makeup of the Republican minority in the House, but they had to bite their tongues, since seniority eventually brought him to the position of senior Republican on the vastly powerful House Appropriations Committee.

Initially a supporter of the Vietnam War, he changed his mind in the late 1960s. Was this change signaled by a brief speech buried in *The Congressional Record*? Not for a minute—that wasn't Silvio Conte's way. He went home to Massachusetts and announced his newly evolved position against the war in front of a dumbfounded and extremely unhappy veterans' group. His regret concerning his vote for the infamous Tonkin Gulf Resolution, during the Vietnam War, eventually led him to vote against the resolution giving President Bush authority to wage the Gulf War against Iraq.

With this stalwart vote against a president of his own party only recently behind him, Silvio Conte died of complications from prostate cancer on February 9, 1991, at the beginning of his seventeenth successive term in the Congress of the United States.

A Double First

●▬●▬●▬●▬●▬●▬●▬●▬●▬●▬●▬●▬●▬●▬●

T HE BLOND WOMAN IN the simple but stylish white suit
walked forward across the high platform toward the po-
dium. The thousands of people in the huge convention hall
below her were on their feet cheering and applauding—simply
roaring with excitement. The woman's trademark smile, big
and warm, broadened as she waved to the multitudes receiving
her with such high emotions, many of their faces streaked with
tears even as they beamed with joy. And across the country,
tens of millions of Americans watched with similar excitement
as their television sets brought this extraordinary moment into
their living rooms. Geraldine Ferraro was about to make her
acceptance speech as the first woman ever nominated by a
major political party to run for the office of vice president of
the United States.

In millions of households across the country there was a
special sense of pride—not only was Geraldine Ferraro the
first woman to be nominated on a major ticket, she was also
the first Italian American. The three-term Representative from
Queens, New York, mother of three, was carrying a lot of
hopes as she strode into the national spotlight. But neither the
man who had chosen her, Democratic presidential nominee
Walter F. Mondale, nor the man who had strongly urged her

choice, Speaker of the House Thomas P. O'Neill, had any doubts that Gerry Ferraro could live up to the burden being placed on her. No one who knew Gerry Ferraro doubted her abilities.

Born on August 26, 1935, this was a woman who did not believe in obstacles. She was the only daughter of a successful restaurant owner, Dominick Ferraro, and his indomitable wife, Antonetta. Three of the couple's four sons had died before they reached the age of three, and Dominick himself died of a heart attack when Geraldine was not yet nine. Antonetta had had to return to crocheting beadwork in a garment factory, but she saw to it that her daughter got a first-class education. And Gerry Ferraro made the most of it, going on from Marymount Manhattan College to earn a law degree at Fordham University—one of two women in her class—while teaching second grade to support herself. In a telling example of Ferraro's intelligence, organization, hard work, and unflappability, she passed the notoriously difficult New York Bar exam on her first try in the same week that she was married to businessman John Zaccaro in a full, formal ceremony.

For the next dozen years, Ferraro was chiefly a mother to her three children, but she then decided that the time had come to do more with her life and put her law degree to real work. When a cousin, Nicholas Ferraro, was elected Queens district attorney in 1974, she passed a screening panel and was selected as one of more than eighty new assistant D.A.s. She specialized in cases involving abused children, and became known for her hard work and ability to operate as a team player. In 1978 an opportunity presented itself to run for the House of Representatives when the long-term incumbent unexpectedly decided to retire because of age. No one thought she had a chance to win—but she did, and was twice reelected before being tapped for the vice-presidential spot on the Democratic ticket. It was not just her warmth and outgoing political style that brought her the nod, however. In the House as in the Queens district attorney's office, she was a team player—an unusual trait in someone as smart, talented, and clearly ambitious as Ferraro.

The fall election went to a seemingly unbeatable Ronald Reagan, but Ferraro had brought enormous grace under pressure and a real pizzazz to the Democratic ticket. She held up under tough, almost abusive, questioning about her husband's finances, and more than held her own in debate with Vice President Bush.

To many voters, she was the best thing about the campaign, and her strong presence made it a certainty that there would be more women on national tickets in years to come. She had been the first, shown the way, and had done nothing to dampen the future for other women at the highest levels of national politics. You do not necessarily have to win to achieve a triumph, to become a symbol of what can be.

Elected by the People

B ELOW IS A LIST of distinguished Italian-American political
figures. Connect the name in the left-hand column with
the correct political office listed in the right-hand column.

1. Michael V. DiSalle	a. Ohio Governor 1983–1991
2. Richard F. Celeste	b. Rhode Island Senator 1950–1976
3. Albert D. Rosellini	c. New York Governor 1983–
4. John O. Pastore	d. Arizona Senator 1977–
5. Mario M. Cuomo	e. Massachusetts Governor 1957–1960
6. Foster Furcolo	f. New Jersey Governor 1990–
7. Dennis DeConcini	g. Washington Governor 1957–1964
8. James J. Florio	h. Ohio Governor 1959–1962
9. John A. Volpe	i. Massachusetts Governor 1965–1969

Answers: 1–h; 2–a; 3–g; 4–b; 5–c; 6–e; 7–d; 8–f; 9–i.

A Master of Tension

●▬●▬●▬●▬●▬●▬●▬●▬●▬●▬●▬●▬●▬●▬●▬●

T HE MOVIE SEEMS TO be over. What else can possibly happen? Well, the ground can begin to tremble and pulsate, and then simply tear itself apart, and up out of this abyss can reach the arms of Sissy Spacek, relentlessly haunting the dreams of Amy Irving, lone survivor of Spacek's revenge. This final image from Brian De Palma's riveting movie of the Stephen King novel *Carrie* is one of those scenes that many moviegoers can never quite get out of their minds.

Carrie made Brian De Palma a major director on the Hollywood scene. He had already made several movies, most of them very low budget, and one of them, 1973's *Sisters*, was almost as terrifying as *Carrie*. But *Carrie* was a huge hit in 1976, and from then on Brian De Palma was listed in the top rank of Hollywood directors. He was also from then on regularly accused by some critics of aping Hitchcock, but with more gore thrown in. De Palma is perfectly willing to admit a debt to Hitchcock, but in fact, he is very much his own man, one of the great technicians of his time with a nervy, unsettling style of camera movement and editing that is distinctly his own.

Born in Newark, New Jersey, September 11, 1940, De Palma was fascinated by movies from an early age. He graduated from Columbia and then earned an M.A. at Sarah Lawrence, where he made his first short, *Woton's Wake*, which won several awards. His style was already evident in his second feature film, *Greetings* (1968), an offbeat comedy made for practically nothing that introduced Robert De Niro to the screen and which won the Silver Bear at the 1969 Berlin Film Festival.

It was *Carrie* that gave De Palma his commercial break-through in 1976, but another movie released the same year, *Obsession*, was actually more typical of his later work, as it peeled away layer upon layer of appearances to arrive at a horrific truth. De Palma's movies are sufficiently complex that they bear repeated viewings, whether the subject is a trans-vestite murderer (*Dressed to Kill*, 1980) or a Vietnam massacre (*Casualties of War*, 1989). Perhaps because he is full of sur-prises, he has had both major hits and major flops over the years. But the flops, like 1990's *Bonfire of the Vanities*, which was under widespread attack in the press because of its casting even before the cameras began to roll, are actually more in-teresting than some of the biggest hits, like 1987's *The Un-touchables*.

There have always been a few critics who seem to keep a special knife sharpened in their desk drawers for Brian De Palma, and use it with a vengeance if given the slightest op-portunity. But De Palma is an artist, not a Hollywood hack, and he just goes right on to making the next film with which to haunt our dreams.

Opera as Theater

•━•━•━•━•━•━•━•━•━•━•━•━•━•━•━•

NO OPERATIC WORK EVER composed has been seen by more
people—untold millions—than *Amahl and the Night
Visitors*, commissioned for television by NBC and first presented at Christmastime in 1951. It became a Christmas tradition and was broadcast year after year into the 1970s. Its
composer, Gian-Carlo Menotti, had already proved himself
capable of attracting a very different audience to opera. His
double bill of *The Medium* and *The Telephone* (1947) was the
first opera production ever presented for an extended run on
Broadway. It lasted for 211 performances, but he did even
better with 1950's *The Consul*, which won the Pulitzer Prize
for music and had a Broadway run of 269 performances in
1950.

Menotti, born near Milan on July 7, 1911, came to the
United States in 1927. He has always had the gift of telling
stories of such inherent drama that audiences were willing to
accept an operatic score even when they were not usual opera
fans. *The Saint of Bleecker Street* did not have as long a Broadway run, but brought Menotti another Pulitzer in 1955. A
man of broad talents, he also wrote the librettos for and directed
most of his operas. He also wrote the libretto for and directed

composer Samuel Barber's *Vanessa*, which premiered at the Metropolitan Opera in 1958.

Beginning in 1958, Menotti ran a performing arts festival in the ancient Italian hill town of Spoleto, which attracted visitors from all over the world. The festival was transplanted to Charleston, South Carolina, in the 1980s, where Menotti is still going strong in his eighties.

Not all music critics have been willing to consider his works as compositions of the first rank, but there is little question that Menotti did as much as anyone to broaden the audience for opera from the middle of the century to the present.

Prima Ballerina

●▬●▬●▬●▬●▬●▬●▬●▬●▬●▬●▬●▬●▬●

THE DARK-HAIRED GIRL FROM Evanston, Illinois, was only fifteen when she made her professional debut with Ballets U.S.A. in 1961, a year that brought a tour of Europe and a performance at the Kennedy White House. A year later she joined the New York City Ballet, whose school she had attended, as a member of the corps, and became a soloist in 1965. In 1969 she was named a prima ballerina, and throughout the 1970s danced principal roles in the world premier of one new George Balanchine work after another, including *Tschaikovsky Suite #3* (1970), PAMTGG (1971), *Union Jack* (1976), and *Vienna Waltzes* (1977).

Although Kay Mazzo had the typically strong technical resources of a Balanchine prima ballerina, she tended to stand out because of the emotional force of her personality. She was particularly admired by critics from the start and became a great audience favorite as well.

Married with two children, Kay Mazzo retired from the stage in 1980, but her legacy is still much apparent at the New York City Ballet, at whose school she has been one of the leading teachers for the last dozen years.

A Style of Her Own

SEXY? WELL, SHE ALWAYS was, but Susan Sarandon is one of those rare actresses who has become more attractive and more provocative as she has aged.

Talented? Two Oscar nominations—for *Atlantic City* (1980) and *Thelma and Louise* (1991)—and a host of critics' and film-festival awards as Best Actress attest to that. Once again, she seems to keep getting better and better.

Unconventional? One of the most intelligent actresses in the business, she has never been afraid to express her opinions, whether on *The Tonight Show* or in magazine interviews. She has two children by actor Tim Robbins, who costarred opposite her in the 1988 hit *Bull Durham*, but they have not married. Sarandon has never been the kind of actress who has worried about crafting a public "image." She clearly knows who she is, and if there are people who don't like her, fine.

Born to Philip Leslie and Leonora Marie Criscione Tomalin on October 4, 1946, in New York City, Sarandon's professional name comes from her early marriage to actor Chris Sarandon, whom she met when they were both pursuing drama degrees at Catholic University in Washington, D.C.

She became a Ford model and then began acting on television, appearing in the soap opera *Search for Tomorrow* and a number of drama specials. She also acquired considerable stage experience. She then attracted considerable notice in the cult classic *The Rocky Horror Picture Show*, but her film career did not really begin to take off until Louis Malle cast her as Brooke Shields's prostitute mother in 1978's controversial *Pretty Baby*.

Throughout her career, Sarandon has shown a remarkable versatility, able to create equally convincing women in films ranging from the satirical comedies *Compromising Positions* (1985) and *The Witches of Eastwick* (1987), to a gritty drama about apartheid, *A Dry White Season* (1989), to an arty horror movie, *The Hunger* (1983), in which she was a memorably dangerous vampire recruit. Susan Sarandon has become that rare creature, an actress so interesting and compelling that it is worth watching even her flops just for her performance.

The Saga of a Family

●━●

THE HEAVYSET MAN WHO suddenly burst into the limelight
in 1969 had been on the fringes of the literary world for
years. He'd written a lot of book reviews for various publica-
tions, published three well-reviewed novels that few people
bought, and had been editor of *Male* magazine. Born in New
York City on October 15, 1920, educated at Columbia University and the New School for Social Research in New York,
he was forty-nine in 1969, an age at which a lot of writers
who have never tasted fame or fortune begin to think maybe
they ought to throw in the towel.

Not Mario Puzo—he was just hitting his stride. His new
novel, *The Godfather*, shot to the top of the best-seller lists
and stayed there for months. It was number one for twenty-
two weeks, and would have been there much longer if people
hadn't bought it in such huge quantities. Never before had a
book leaped off the printing presses into readers' eager hands
at such a pace. But then, nobody had written about the "Mafia"
this way before. The novel was gritty and violent, but it was
also the story of a particular family, characters who came to
life as real people who could be cared about in spite of their
bloody hands. Even Italian Americans who had spent years
fighting the stereotype of Italians as mobsters found it difficult

to resist the saga of Don Corleone and his family. Although Puzo said that he had used many stories he had heard over the years from relatives and friends, he admitted that he hadn't, so far as he knew, ever met a real mob member in his life, and had had to do extensive research for the book. Puzo was first of all a novelist, a close observer of the human condition with masterful story-telling instincts.

The Godfather was an inevitable movie subject, but by the kind of pure chance that makes for Hollywood legend, the young director assigned to it, Francis Ford Coppola, was so perfectly attuned to the material that what was orginally viewed by studio executives as just another gangster movie was elevated to the realms of movie greatness. Puzo and Coppola collaborated on the screenplay, which brought them the 1972 Academy Award for Best Screenplay based on material from another medium, while the film itself was named Best Picture, and made $86.3 million in North America alone, establishing itself as the sixth-highest-grossing movie of the decade.

In 1974 Puzo won a second writing Oscar with Coppola for *The Godfather, Part II* (and the film was also named Best Picture of that year), and then went on to script such blockbuster movies as *Earthquake* (1974), *Superman* (1979), and *Superman II* (1980). He and Coppola were again nominated for Best Screenplay for *Godfather III* (1990). The three *Godfather* films are widely regarded by critics as one of the most ambitious and fully realized achievements in Hollywood history.

An Epic Achievement

●▬●▬●▬●▬●▬●▬●▬●▬●▬●▬●▬●▬●▬●

Q. How many Academy Award nominations has Francis Ford Coppola received as director, screenwriter, or producer?

   a. 9
   b. 12
   c. 14

A. The answer is b.

Q. For what 1970 Best Picture did he receive his first nomination (as screenwriter) and his first gold statue?

A. *Patton.* He cowrote the screenplay with Edmund H. North.

Q. How many Oscars has Coppola won altogether?

A. Five, the other four all stemming from the first two *Godfather* movies. He won screenplay honors, together with Mario Puzo, for both *The Godfather* and *The Godfather, Part II,* and also received awards as director and producer of the latter. Both movies won the Best Picture award, but he was not the producer of the first one.

Q. All three *Godfather* movies were nominated for Best Picture. Can you name the other two Coppola movies that received nominations for Best Picture?

A. *The Conversation* (1974), in which Gene Hackman portrays an electronic eavesdropping expert who hears far too much for his own good, and the Vietnam War epic *Apocalypse Now* (1979)

Q. *Apocalypse Now* won the top prize at the Cannes Film Festival, the Palme d'Or. What other film of his also won at Cannes?

A. *The Conversation,* which some critics feel is his finest film, although it has been eclipsed by the *Godfather* series.

Q. Coppola wrote and directed two movies in 1983 based on the novels of S. E. Hinton, *The Outsiders* and *Rumble Fish.* How many of the following actors made their screen debuts in these two films?
Tom Cruise
Matt Dillon
Rob Lowe
Mickey Rourke
Nicolas Cage
Patrick Swayze
Ralph Macchio
Emilio Estevez

A. All of them did.

Q. How many relatives has Coppola used in important roles in his films?

A. Three. His sister, Talia Shire, played Michael Corleone's sister in all three *Godfather* films, receiving a nomination as Best Supporting Actress for *The Godfather, Part II.* (She was nominated for Best Actress for the non-Coppola *Rocky,* 1976.) Shire also appeared in the Coppola segment of the three-part 1989 *New York Stories.* Coppola's nephew Nicolas Cage was in *Rumble Fish,* and became a star in the Coppola-directed *Peggy Sue Got Married* (1986). Coppola's daughter Sofia was a last-minute replacement for Winona Ryder in *Godfather III.* She was widely attacked by critics, although a few more objective ones thought she did a fine job.

Q. Coppola's father, Carmine, has written the score for many of his son's films. What kind of musical training did he receive?

A. The best; he studied both flute and composition at Juilliard and the Manhattan School of Music and was a flutist under Toscanini for the NBC orchestra. He won the Oscar, together with Nino Rota, for their music for *The Godfather, Part II.*

Q. Can you name two movies starring Mickey Rooney for which Coppola was executive producer?

A. *The Black Stallion* (1979) and *The Black Stallion Returns* (1983).

Q. Name the immensely popular 1973 movie about the 1950s produced by Coppola that proved a breakthrough movie for another director who has since become a Hollywood legend in his own right.

A. George Lucas's *American Graffiti,* which was nominated for four Academy Awards, including a Best Director nomination for Lucas and a Best Picture nod. Coppola was the first Hollywood director to come out of the UCLA film school (his first feature, *You're a Big Boy Now,* 1966, began as his thesis project), and he has always been extremely generous in promoting the work of his fellow graduates.

Q. Can you name Coppola's two most expensive flops?

A. *One from the Heart* (1982), which cost twenty-eight million dollars, and *The Cotton Club* (1984), which cost forty-eight million.

Q. Despite Coppola's ups and downs, is there any Hollywood director of the last twenty-five years whom critics regard as more influential?

A. No, not even Lucas or Spielberg. The *Godfather* series alone is regarded as a unique achievement in film history.

"Cut Me and I'll Bleed Dodger Blue"

••••••••••••••••••••••••••••••••••••••

HOW DO YOU GET to be a World Championship baseball manager? Well, after serving in the army from 1945 to 1947, you could become a minor-league pitcher, and finally make it to the big leagues for three pretty lousy years, two with the Brooklyn Dodgers 1954 to 1955, and one with the Kansas City A's, 1956. Then, since your pitching prowess leaves a lot to be desired, you could become a minor-league manager in the Dodgers organization, practicing your craft in places like Pocatello, Idaho, and Ogden, Utah, and on to triple-A ball in Spokane and Albuquerque. And then having more than paid your dues, you could get called up to manage the Dodgers themselves—and become only the second National League manager to win the pennant your first two years in a row, in 1977 and 1978. Your name of course, would be Tom Charles Lasorda, known to everyone as Tommy.

Born in Norristown, Pennsylvania, on September 22, 1927, Lasorda has proved himself one of the most successful managers in baseball history, and has led the Dodgers for an astonishing sixteen years since being called up in the middle of the 1976 season. Lasorda's Los Angeles Dodgers were beaten by the New York Yankees in the first two World Series he managed, in 1977 and 1978, four games to two both times.

But the Dodgers turned the tables in 1981, downing the Yankees four to two. They were out of the World Series for a while, sometimes in contention, sometimes not, but came back in 1988 to beat Oakland four games to one. Tommy Lasorda was named Manager of the Year in 1988.

One of the most colorful men in the game, the loquacious manager's nonstop spiels once caused Joe Garagiola to comment while broadcasting a game, "You can plant two thousand rows of corn with the fertilizer Lasorda spreads around." Lasorda pays no attention to such comments. He just comes back with more of the same: "Managing is like holding a dove in your hand. Squeeze too hard and you kill it; not hard enough and it flies away."

A "New York Actor"

●▬●▬●▬●▬●▬●▬●▬●▬●▬●▬●▬●▬●▬●▬●▬●

HOW MANY ACADEMY AWARD nominations can an actor pile up without ever winning? The record is seven, shared by Peter O'Toole and the late Richard Burton. Paul Newman had racked up six before he finally snagged the elusive trophy for *The Color of Money*. Al Pacino is now up to six, too. His first was a supporting nomination for his role as the reluctant heir to the mantle of family leader in *The Godfather* (1972). The next year he was nominated for Best Actor as the incorruptible New York cop in *Serpico*. In 1974 and 1975 there were two more Best Actor nominations for *The Godfather, Part II*, and for the utterly different role of a crazed bank robber in *Dog Day Afternoon. And Justice for All* brought him still another chance at Oscar in 1979. During the 1980s he made fewer and less successful movies, but was again nominated for Best Supporting Actor for his wild comic turn in 1990's *Dick Tracy*. Many thought he should also have been nominated for Best Actor that year for his role as the despairing Don in the climactic *The Godfather, Part III*, and were sure he would at least get the Supporting Actor award as recompense. No such luck.

There are those who speculate that Pacino's problem in copping an Oscar is that he is a "New York Actor," rather than a "Hollywood Star." Born in New York City on April 25, 1940, Pacino attended the High School for the Performing Arts, and went on to study acting at the Herbert Berghof Studio and the Actors Studio. He first came to major public attention in 1968 in *The Indian Wants the Bronx*, for which he won the Off-Broadway Best Actor Obie award. The next year, he won a Tony as Best Supporting Actor in *Does a Tiger Wear a Necktie?*

In 1969, he began his film career, but has regularly returned to the New York theater, winning the Best Actor Tony in 1977 for *The Basic Training of Pavlo Hummel*. His stage roles are often offbeat choices, such as the gangster/king in Brecht's *The Rise of Arturo Ui*, and King Herod in Oscar Wilde's *Salome* in 1992. Such choices may alienate members of the Hollywood community for whom the words "stage classic" are synonymous with "pretentious," and it may be that that attitude will forever deny Pacino an Oscar. But he has been widely named as Best Actor by critics' groups down through the years, and the lack of an Oscar will certainly not prevent him from being regarded as one of the preeminent actors of his time.

Mr. Musical—and a Lot More Besides

T HE SCENES REVERBERATE IN the memory of every movie
fan: Judy Garland singing on a trolley (*Meet Me in St.
Louis*, 1944); Spencer Tracy taking a nightmare walk down a
church aisle that rolls beneath his feet (*Father of the Bride*,
1950); Gene Kelly and Leslie Caron dancing through an Im-
pressionistic Paris (*An American in Paris*, 1951); Kirk Douglas
in a frenzy of painting (*Lust for Life*, 1956); Maurice Chevalier
thanking Heaven for little girls in a Paris park (*Gigi*, 1958);
Shirley MacLaine shot to death amid a roiling carnival crowd
(*Some Came Running*, 1958).

Vincente Minnelli was the director of all these movies and
a couple dozen more, many of them equally memorable. From
the mid–1940s through the early 1960s, he was one of Hollywood's most versatile, successful, and prolific directors, and
without question, the preeminent director of film musicals.

Born in Chicago on February 28, 1910, he came from a
family that toured a tent show through the Midwest. He started
out in the entertainment business in Chicago, designing sets
and costumes and moved on to do the same in New York
beginning in 1931. There he met with quick success and was
soon designing Radio City Music Hall extravaganzas, and took

another step forward directing Broadway musicals starting in 1935.

In the early 1940s, Arthur Freed of MGM was putting together a special unit under his command to make musicals, and he made Minnelli a crucial part of that endeavor. Minnelli's first directorial job at MGM was the all-black musical *Cabin in the Sky*, a risky venture that he turned into a great success in 1943. And following *Meet Me in St. Louis* the next year, there was no stopping him.

Q. Which of the following musicals did Vincente Minnelli *not* direct?

a. *The Pirate*, 1948
b. *Brigadoon*, 1954
c. *Funny Face*, 1957
d. *Bells Are Ringing*, 1960
e. *On a Clear Day You Can See Forever*, 1970

A. The answer is c, which was directed by Stanley Donen, Minnelli's only main competition in the field of musicals.

Despite being especially associated with musicals, Minnelli was also a first-rate director of strong dramatic—even melodramatic—movies: *Madame Bovary* (1949), with Jennifer Jones very fine in the title role; *The Bad and the Beautiful* (1952), an acerbic inside look at Hollywood with Kirk Douglas and Lana Turner; the mental-institution thriller *The Cobweb* (1955); and *Home from the Hill* (1959), the dark story of a doomed Southern family, starring Robert Mitchum and introducing both George Hamilton and George Peppard as his warring sons—all were critical and box office successes.

The apex of Minnelli's career was 1958. Not only did *Gigi* win for Best Picture, but it garnered eight other Oscars, including Best Director for Minnelli himself. But that wasn't all. His other big success of that year, *Some Came Running*, picked up Oscar nominations in three of the four acting categories, for Shirley MacLaine as Best Actress and Arthur Kennedy and Martha Hyer in the supporting categories. The two movies could hardly be more different, and stand as memorable testimony to the great talents of Vincente Minnelli, who knew how to make the most of almost any project he was called upon to direct.

"With a Z"

As the daughter of the legendary Judy Garland and the first-rank director Vincente Minnelli, you would expect Liza Minnelli to have talent. But it is hardly an easy task to live up to the memory of Judy Garland, and the fact that Liza has succeeded is even more to her credit.

She made her first movie appearance at the age of two and a half at the end of her mother's movie *In the Good Old Summertime* (1949). By the age of seventeen she was appearing Off Broadway in the revival of *Best Foot Forward.* The following year she sang with her mother during Garland's run at the London Palladium, and in 1965 starred on Broadway in the musical *Flora the Red Menace* by John Kander and Fred Ebb, with whom she formed a lifelong creative relationship. The role brought her the Tony Award as Best Actress in a Musical, the youngest ever to have won the award.

Her first movie since she was a toddler was 1967's *Charlie Bubbles* with Albert Finney, which gave immediate evidence that she could shine even if she wasn't singing. Neither *The Sterile Cuckoo* (1969) nor *Tell Me That You Love Me, Junie Moon* (1970) were big successes at the box office, but the first gained her a nomination for Best Actress and both performances were greeted with strong praise from critics. Then in

"Miss Show Business," Liza Minnelli, striking her classic pose as she belts out a song in Paris AFP

1972 came *Cabaret*, a major box office success that is also considered by many critics to be one of the two best musicals ever made, along with *Singin' in the Rain*. Liza won the Oscar for Best Actress and numerous other awards for the role that she had nearly landed when the show lit up the Broadway season five years earlier in 1967. At the time, director Harold Prince had finally decided that she was too young and not quite ready, and she was the first to admit in retrospect that he had been right. By 1972, however, she was more than ready.

Liza's subsequent movie career has had its ups and downs, largely because of problems in finding the right vehicles for her talents. She was a knockout in 1977's *New York, New York*, and her rendition of the title song can work an audience into a frenzy to this day. In 1981, *Arthur* was a huge popular success, but she has since concentrated more on her concert career, with sell-out engagements in some of the biggest theaters in the world, including a two-week engagement in 1991 at Radio City Music Hall.

Along the way, Liza collected a second Tony Award for the Broadway musical *The Act* (1977); a Tony nomination for *The Rink* (1984); both an Emmy and a Grammy for her highly acclaimed 1972 television special *Liza with a Z* (in which she memorably explains how to spell her first name)—and despite a sometimes troubled personal life, she has become one of those rare performers whom everybody refers to by her first name.

Liza Minnelli was always close to her mother and father, and has more than made good on the unique genes her extraordinary parents passed on to her.

Roles Chosen
with Care

•—•—•—•—•—•—•—•—•—•—•—•—•—•—•—•—•—•

H E WAS A NONE-TOO-BRIGHT major-league catcher with a
terminal disease (*Bang the Drum Slowly*, 1973; Best Actor, New York Film Critics).

He played Don Corleone as a young man, managing in a
very subtle way to suggest that he would indeed become the
old man played by Marlon Brando in *The Godfather* (*The
Godfather, Part II*, 1974; Academy Award for Best Supporting
Actor).

He was a deranged, violent, but terribly human loner who
could not abide the world around him (*Taxi Driver*, 1976;
nominated for Best Actor Oscar).

He held together, almost single-handedly, a long, complex
film that won the Oscar as Best Picture, even though his role
as a Pennsylvania steelworker turned Vietnam Green Beret
was highly ambiguous—an almost impossible task that he carried off (*The Deer Hunter*, 1978; nominated for Best Actor
Oscar).

He dug deep into the tortured soul of boxer Jake La Motta,
garnering understanding and sympathy for an unlikable character (*Raging Bull*, 1980; Best Actor Oscar).

Equally effective as a crazed amateur stand-up comic (*The
King of Comedy*, 1983), a slave trader converted to Jesuit mis-

sionary (*The Mission*, 1986), a patient brought back from a coma after twenty years (*Awakenings*, 1990), or an ex-con out for revenge against his lawyer (*Cape Fear*, 1991, Best Actor nomination), Robert De Niro is one of the most versatile and respected screen actors of his time.

Born August 17, 1943, in New York City, the son of two painters prominent in New York art circles, De Niro's life has been acting, in a way more common among stage actors than movie stars. He was trained by the legendary Stella Adler and Lee Strasberg and began his career on the Off-Broadway stage. His name is seldom in the gossip columns and he gives few interviews. But he is far from being a loner: His TriBeCa Film Center in New York City is at the center of film-making activity in the city, and he is a continuing champion of new talent.

While never a star of the kind guaranteed to bring in the box-office gold, he has probably made more films of lasting quality than any other screen actor of his generation. That may be because he knows how to read a script. Nobody has made better choices than Robert De Niro.

A Most Fortunate Man

•◄●◄●◄●◄●◄●◄●◄●◄●◄●◄●◄●◄●◄●◄●

THERE IS AN ANCIENT Italian belief—which may derive from the seven hills of Rome—that the seventh son of a seventh son will be a most fortunate man. That certainly proved to be the case for Pierino Roland Como, born on May 18, 1912, into a family that would eventually number thirteen children. His father, Pietro, a millhand, and his mother, Lucia, raised their close-knit family to look out for one another and at the same time to develop self-sufficiency. Pierino, who would come to be called Perry, began to make his way in the world early, opening a barbershop at the age of fourteen, where he cut hair after school every afternoon and all day on Saturday.

Expanding to a full-time schedule after he graduated from high school, Perry was making a then princely sum of one hundred dollars a week. But on a visit to Cleveland with friends, he was talked into auditioning for the bandleader Freddy Carlone. He was immediately offered a job, at twenty-eight dollars a week. His parents told him to take it—he could always go back to barbering. Within a year he was touring with the better-known Ted Weems band, and had married his childhood sweetheart, Roselle Belline.

When the Ted Weems Band broke up in 1942, thirty-year-old Perry Como took to the radio airwaves and landed an RCA

Victor recording contract. His smooth voice and amiable personality brought him more and more fans. He became a New York nightclub favorite at the Versailles and the Copacabana, and proved that he could wow a younger set as well with a hugely successful stint at the Paramount Theater.

From his first hit single, "Goodbye Sue," in 1943, through such million-sellers as "Till the End of Time" and "It's Impossible," Como developed a following that would stick with him through the decades no matter how musical tastes changed. His appearances five nights a week on NBC radio's *Chesterfield Supper Club* kept his fans tuned in from 1944 to 1955; they followed happily when the show went from fifteen minutes nightly to a half hour weekly in 1949 so that it could be simultaneously broadcast on the new medium of television. In 1955, he signed an unprecedented twelve-year contract with NBC television and Kraft Foods; Perry Como's *Kraft Music Hall* was number one in its time slot for years, and brought him Emmy Awards in 1954, 1955, and 1956.

Beginning in the late 1960s, Como turned to performing at Las Vegas, making yearly cross-country concert tours, and an annual television Christmas special. In 1991, at the age of seventy-nine, he was still packing them in with a Christmas tour. Although he had always won his share of awards, including the very first Grammy for Best Male Vocal in 1958 for "Catch a Falling Star," special recognition of his lifetime achievements came with increasing frequency in recent years. He was one of the five recipients of the Kennedy Center Honors in 1987 and was elected to the Television Hall of Fame in 1990.

Married to Roselle for more than fifty years, with three children, thirteen grandchildren, and one great-grandchild, still singing mellifluously as he enters his eighties, Perry Como can indeed count himself among the most fortunate of men.

Follow These Steps

••••••••••••••••••••••••••••••

"A DANCER DANCES," GOES the lyric from A *Chorus Line*, which is what Peter Gennaro decided to do. He was born in Metairie, Louisiana, a suburb of New Orleans, in 1924, and took dance lessons throughout his childhood. But he was working in his father's New Orleans bar when he made up his mind, following World War II, that he'd be "better off tapping floors than beer," and used the GI Bill to further his dance studies. After an initial stint with the San Carlo Opera Company, he quickly gravitated to Broadway and from 1949 to 1956 appeared in many of the major musicals of the period, including *Kiss Me Kate, Guys and Dolls, Pajama Game*, and *Bells Are Ringing*.

Married to former ballet dancer Jean Kinsella, he began to turn his attention to the more secure life afforded a good choreographer, and proved to be one of the best. The first show he choreographed, *Seventh Heaven* (1955), was one of those expected hits that turn out to be a flop, although he himself got good notices. There would be many more Broadway shows to come, the second one, *West Side Story*, proving to be a huge success. Gennaro was its co-choreographer with Jerome Robbins, who conceived and directed the show. On his own, Gennaro lent his sizzling talents as choreographer to such long-running hits as *Fiorello!* (1959) and *Annie* (1977), for which he won the Tony Award.

But the majority of Gennaro's time was spent working in the medium of television, where he was unquestionably its foremost choreographer, working with many of the biggest names in show business, including the weekly shows of Andy Williams, Perry Como, Judy Garland, and Bing Crosby. His work popped up everywhere, from Ed Sullivan specials to the Academy Awards to Radio City Music Hall, where he served as choreographer for many years.

Capable of working in a wide range of styles, and a complete professional known for his steady hand and ability to work with anyone, Peter Gennaro has communicated his zest and inventiveness to hundreds of thousands of theatergoers and untold millions of television viewers.

A Whirlwind of Dance

●▬●▬●▬●▬●▬●▬●▬●▬●▬●▬●▬●▬●●

FOR THIRTY YEARS, THE ballets created by Gerald Arpino for the Joffrey Ballet have been causing excitement among dance audiences across the country and around the world. The titles of many of these ballets are alone sufficient to convey the buoyancy and speed of many of his creations: *Viva Vivaldi, Olympics, Fanfarita, L'Air d'Esprit, Celebration, Jamboree.* These works have served to show off the special quickness and airborn élan of three generations of Joffrey dancers. As bodies hurtled across the stage in variation after variation, audiences were often left nearly breathless with joy at these explosions of sustained movement.

Arpino himself had been a dancer with the company from 1956 to 1962, following a year spent with the Ballet Russe. Born January 14, 1928, in Staten Island, New York, he studied briefly at Wagner College, which awarded him an honorary degree in 1980, and then turned full time to dance studies. In his last year as a dancer with the Joffrey, he choreographed his first ballet for the company, *Incubus.* He taught at the Joffrey Ballet School beginning in 1953, but with the great success of his ballets was named a co-director along with the company's founder, Robert Joffrey. His choreography was a perfect complement to the more romantic ballets of Joffrey himself. It was the addition of Arpino's ballets to the repertoire that led to its development into a leading international company.

Although Arpino is especially celebrated for his bravura full-company ballets, his range as choreographer is wide, and he has also mounted successful works with darker, more introspective themes. From *Viva Vivaldi* on, his works have often created a sensation at their first performances. Ballet lovers who have attended opening nights of ballets such as *The Clowns, Trinity,* or *Kettentanz* have never forgotten that heady experience of being part of an audience simply swept away with excitement.

Gerald Arpino, who had long served as associate director, was named director of the Joffrey following the death of Robert Joffrey in 1988. Although like so many American dance and theater companies the Joffrey has experienced financial difficulties in recent years, Arpino continues to produce ballets that are "must-see" experiences for an enthralled public.

Twice Famous

●◆●◆●◆●◆●◆●◆●◆●◆●◆●◆●◆●◆●

IT IS VERY RARE for a Hollywood leading man to become a household name twice in a lifetime, but that is exactly what was accomplished by Dominic Felix Amici, better known as Don Ameche.

Born in Kenosha, Wisconsin, on May 31, 1908, he started out hoping to become a lawyer, but eventually made his way to Hollywood by way of radio and stage performances. He became a very popular romantic leading man in the 1930s and 1940s, playing opposite Alice Faye a number of times, and also portraying such historic figures as Alexander Graham Bell (in *The Story of Alexander Graham Bell*, 1939), Stephen Foster (in *Swanee River*, 1939), and Diamond Jim Brady (*Lillian Russell*, 1940).

By the end of the 1940s, his box-office appeal evaporated as the movies took on tougher postwar subjects. He continued acting, primarily on stage, and also as a guest star on television, yet made only five movies between 1949 and 1985. Then he was cast as one of the elderly Florida citizens rejuvenated by contact with alien beings in the hit comedy *Cocoon*. All his charm was still intact, he had retained a remarkably good figure, and his athletic antics brought him an Academy Award as Best Supporting Actor, forty-nine years after his first movie.

He went on to star in *Harry and the Hendersons,* 1987, *Cocoon, the Return,* 1988, but was most delighted with his leading role in David Mamet's 1988 movie *Things Change.* For the first time in his life he got to play an Italian, an elderly immigrant shoemaker who agrees to impersonate a mobster. The accent, Ameche said, was a snap; he just remembered his father.

The Italian Navigator
of the Twentieth
Century

●◖●◖●◖●◖●◖●◖●◖●◖●◖●◖●◖●◖●◖●◖●◖●◖●

> **Q.** "Some recent work by E. Fermi and L. Szilard which has been communicated to me in a manuscript, leads me to expect that the element uranium may be turned into a new and important source of energy in the near future." Who wrote these words in a letter to President Roosevelt at the beginning of August 1939?
>
> **A.** They were written by Albert Einstein, who had been enlisted to alert Roosevelt to the vastly important work of Fermi, Szilard, and other physicists—work that could lead to "bombs of a new type and immense power." The letter was hand-delivered to Roosevelt by the economist Alexander Sachs, who was a longtime advisor to Roosevelt and also a friend of Leo Szilard. Roosevelt immediately grasped the importance of the subject and appointed an Advisory Committee for Uranium.

B Y THE TIME HE arrived with his wife, Laura, in the United States in December 1938, Enrico Fermi had already achieved what for most scientists would be the pinnacle of their lives, the Nobel Prize in Physics for 1938. The citation read: "To Enrico Fermi of Rome for his identification of new radioactive elements produced by neutron bombardment and his discovery, made in connection with this work, of nuclear reactions effected by slow neutrons."

Born on September 29, 1901, into a farming family living in the Po Valley of northern Italy, Enrico was quickly recognized as having a truly exceptional and inquiring mind, and on the basis of a paper he wrote concerning the physics of vibrating strings, he gained a special scholarship to a college in Pisa for superior students. Even in this rarefied intellectual atmosphere he stood out and was allowed to pursue his own experimental agenda. Graduating magna cum laude with a doctorate in physics in 1922, he subsequently worked under the great German physicist Max Born at Göttingen, and then taught at the University of Florence for two years before moving on to the University of Rome to occupy a newly created chair in theoretical physics. Three years later at the age of twenty-eight he became one of the youngest men ever elected to the Royal Academy of Italy.

A guest professorship at the University of Michigan from 1930 to 1931 gave him a new perspective on the effects Mussolini's dictatorship was having in Italy, and he returned to his work in Rome a warier and more socially aware man. Over the next few years he followed up on the work James Chadwick of Britain was doing with neutrons, and that Jean-Frédéric Joliot-Curie and his wife, Irene (daughter of two-time Nobel winner Marie Curie), were doing with artificial radioactivity. (Chadwick won the 1935 Nobel Prize in Physics while the Joliot-Curies shared that year's Nobel in Chemistry.) Working with a number of heavy elements and ultimately uranium, Fermi succeeded in changing one element into another—the ancient dream of the medieval alchemists, although they would have been disappointed that he could not transform lead into gold, since they were too far apart in the periodic table.

Fermi also succeeded in creating element 93, neptunium, the first man-made element (element 100 was subsequently named fermium in his honor). Perhaps most important, he demonstrated that if an element was bombarded with neutrons in a medium such as water, the hydrogen in the water slowed the neutrons so that they were more readily absorbed, which increased the radioactivity of the bombarded element. The theoretical groundwork for the atomic bomb was thus established.

By the time Fermi was awarded the Nobel Prize in 1938, Mussolini, in one of his many emulations of Hitler, began constraining the movement of Jews. Fermi's wife, Laura, was Jewish, and he had to beg for her to be allowed to accompany him to Stockholm for the Nobel ceremonies. They knew they would not be returning to Italy, and although they had to leave everything else behind, there would be the fifty-thousand-dollar prize money to ease resettlement in America.

Working with other scientists at Columbia University upon becoming professor there in 1939, Fermi conceived the idea of a chain reaction using uranium-235, a fissionable isotope that makes up less than 2 percent of uranium, the rest being composed of the isotope uranium-238. Only a chain reaction could produce enough uranium-235 to make a bomb possible. But the production of U-235 would have to be carefully controlled or it could lead to a devastating explosion. Fermi decided that nearly pure blocks of graphite would work best and began designing what would become the first atomic pile—so called because it looked like a pile of blocks.

To carry out these experiments would be vastly expensive, but even the concern expressed by many American scientists and their refugee colleagues that Germany was far ahead in such research succeeded in squeezing only modest funds out of skeptical Washington officials. Then came the letter from

Einstein to Roosevelt, and the situation changed radically. The essential government funds became readily available.

Q. On December 2, 1942, Fermi and his colleagues succeeded in achieving the first self-sustaining chain reaction. Where did it take place?
    a. In a basement laboratory at Columbia University.
    b. In a squash court under the football stadium at the University of Chicago.
    b. In a concrete bunker at Oak Ridge, Tennessee.

A. The answer is b. Fermi had transported his graphite pile to the atomic research facilities at the University of Chicago that summer. Once the new pile had been constructed it took only six weeks to achieve a chain reaction. The administrative head of the research program at Chicago was Nobel Prize–winning physicist Arthur H. Compton, but the atomic pile was Fermi's baby, and when the experiment succeeded, Compton immediately telephoned James B. Conant, Roosevelt's top science advisor and future president of Harvard, saying in prearranged code, "The Italian navigator has set foot in the new world." Conant, wishing to make certain that the reaction was under control, asked, "And how are the natives behaving?" "Very well," replied Compton.

At sites in Hartford, Washington, and Oak Ridge, Tennessee, reactors were built to separate uranium into the fissionable U-235 and plutonium, another fissionable element created out of Fermi's processes. And at Los Alamos, New Mexico, the first two atomic bombs were constructed. At first, Fermi moved back and forth among the three sites, but then settled in with the extraordinary team of scientists under the direction of General Leslie R. Groves and the bomb's principal designer, J. Robert Oppenheimer. The test bomb was exploded on July 16, 1945, and Fermi and Oppenheimer were the first to inspect ground zero in a lead-shielded tank. The devastation stunned even them, and Fermi was among the first to call for the bomb to be used only in unpopulated areas. But that was a political and military decision, and the bombing of Hiroshima and Nagasaki followed in August.

In 1946, Fermi received the highest honor bestowed by the United States Congress on civilians, the Congressional Medal of Merit, and in 1954 was the first recipient of an award by the Atomic Energy Commission, on whose advisory board he served. This award has since been known as the Enrico Fermi Award. A few weeks later, on November 28, he died of cancer, as did so many of the early experimenters with radiation. The work of the "Italian navigator," though, had changed the world forever.

Deeper into the Atom

•❧•❧•❧•❧•❧•❧•❧•❧•❧•❧•❧•❧•

ONE OF ENRICO FERMI'S long-time colleagues, and a Nobel Prize winner himself in 1959 (shared with Owen Chamberlain) for work on the antiproton, Emilio Segrè was born in Tivoli, near Rome, on February 1, 1905. Although only four years younger than Fermi, Segrè studied under Fermi at the University of Rome, where he earned his Ph.D. in 1938. Like Fermi, Segrè fled fascist Italy in 1938. In the United States, he started out as a research assistant at the University of California at Berkeley, but was recruited by Fermi to work on the development of the atomic bomb and was a group leader at Los Alamos from 1943 to 1946. He returned to Berkeley as a full professor in the physics department, a position he held until his retirement in 1972.

Part of the team that worked with Fermi on the discovery of slow neutrons, he was also a codiscoverer of plutonium and two other elements, technetium (atomic number 43) and astatine (number 89). His work with Chamberlain on antiprotons, however, was his crowning research achievement.

More than most of the nuclear physicists of his time, Segrè was also as much a teacher as a research scientist, and his death in 1989 was met by the particular sorrow that former students feel about the passing of someone who opened their minds to new horizons.

Wedded to the Law

•▬•▬•▬•▬•▬•▬•▬•▬•▬•▬•▬•▬•▬•▬•

M ICHAEL ANGELO MUSMANNO WAS a truly remarkable man. Like many sons of immigrant Italians, he started to work when he was very young. Born in 1897 in the coal-mining hills around Pittsburgh, Pennsylvania, he had his first job at fourteen, as a coal loader. But he was exceptionally bright, and continued his schooling, taking night courses for years. He was studying at Georgetown University in Washington, D.C., when America entered World War I, and he returned there after serving in the army infantry, eventually getting his law degree. He gradually gained a total of seven degrees. After serving with great success in a major Philadelphia law firm, his thirst for new experience and further studies took him abroad to Rome, Paris, and London.

Returning to private practice in Pennsylvania, Musmanno soon showed a marked degree of interest in defending those without resources, and in 1927, joined the defense team for the final attempt to prevent the execution of the anarchists Nicola Sacco and Bartolomeo Vanzetti, who had been convicted of murder in 1921. The defense was unsuccessful, but as in the equally famous Lindbergh kidnapping case and the Rosenberg treason case, the facts have never ceased to be argued. In 1939, Musmanno wrote his own book, *After Twelve*

Years, defending the anarchists. By that time, he had served four years in the Pennsylvania General Assembly, and seven years as an elected judge.

World War II found Musmanno serving with distinction in the Navy, earning a Purple Heart and numerous other medals and rising from the rank of lieutenant commander to rear admiral. As both a military governor in southern Italy and as president of the American agency charged with preventing refugees from being forced to return from Austria to their original countries now under Communist domination, he proved himself worthy of being chosen as a judge at the Nuremberg war-crimes trials. Musmanno had also been on the team charged with ascertaining the certainty of Hitler's death, and another of his many books, *Ten Days to Die,* published in 1950, detailed his work questioning several dozen of the people closest to Hitler. All of these experiences led him to become one of the first to call for a World Court to deal with "crimes against humanity." If such a court is ever established, Musmanno would undoubtedly be honored as one of its instigators.

In 1951 he was elected to a twenty-one-year term on the Pennsylvania Supreme Court, which did not prevent him from writing several more books, serving as a prosecution witness at the trial of Adolf Eichmann, and continuing, as he always had, to study and learn more about the law and the world in which he lived.

The law was Michael Musmanno's life—he never married—and he served it with extraordinary distinction. He was still a sitting judge at the time of his death in 1969.

A Vision for
Future Living

●◄●◄●◄●◄●◄●◄●◄●◄●◄●◄●◄●◄●◄●◄●►●

FEW MODERN ARCHITECTS HAVE managed to arouse more interest with so few completed works to their name than Paolo Soleri. As much visionary as architect, Soleri was born in Turin, Italy, on June 21, 1919. He graduated with a doctorate in architecture from Turin Polytechnic in 1946, and first came to the United States the next year on a fellowship from the Frank Lloyd Wright Foundation, working at Taliesin West in Phoenix, Arizona. In 1949 he married Carolyn Woods, and built an unusual and very striking house for her mother, working together with his fellow Wright apprentice Mark Mills. Called the Dome House and located at Cave Creek, Arizona, it remains remarkable to this day.

In 1950, Soleri and his wife moved to Italy, where they became much involved in making ceramics. Near Palermo, Sicily, Soleri designed and built a ceramics workshop, the external walls of which were faced in glazed pots—the entire building making strict use of locally available materials and crafts. Returning to Arizona in 1955, Soleri began the construction of the Cosanti Foundation on a five-acre site near Scottsdale. The workshops at Cosanti are used to make ceramic chimes and metal bells which have served to support the architect's work on visionary blueprints and models for a new kind of urban living with a strong emphasis on ecology. An exhibition of this work toured several major cities in the early 1970s drawing large, astonished crowds. The models for his "bridge cities," urban complexes that would tower into clouds while using a small base of land, looked like something from another planet, very strange yet absolutely wondrous.

In 1970, work was begun near Cordes Junction, Arizona, on a prototype urban community for five thousand people. Since the construction of this community, called Arcosanti, is done largely by summer apprentices and year-round volunteers, the twenty-five-story "town" covering thirteen acres of an eight-hundred-sixty-acre site of breathtaking beauty, is unlikely to be completed until well after the turn of the century, but it is already one of the most remarkable architectural entities on earth. To raise capital, Soleri has traveled and lectured around the world, as well as staging an annual Arts and Music Festival at Arcosanti.

Making use of Soleri's innovative techniques for concrete casting and the very latest ideas in energy conservation, Arcosanti is likely to still be far ahead of its time even when completed. And Soleri has many followers who believe that centuries from now Soleri will be looked back upon as the father of an entirely new way of living on our fragile planet.

A Wonderful Life

•❧•❧•❧•❧•❧•❧•❧•❧•❧•❧•❧•❧•

IN 1903, A SIX-YEAR-OLD BOY from Palermo, Sicily, came to America with his parents. The family made its way to California, where the father found employment as a fruit picker. The boy, whose first name was anglicized as Frank, was exceedingly bright, and after high school he managed, despite a chronic shortage of money, to work his way through the rigorous California Institute of Technology, graduating in 1918 with a degree in chemical engineering. He served in the army in the closing months of World War I, and then returned to California, where he drifted for the next two years. Then in 1922, he wrangled a job directing a movie short called *Fulta Fisher's Boarding House* for a minor film company. The career of one of Hollywood's most celebrated directors, Frank Capra, was under way.

During the next four years, Capra worked in every area of movie-making, from gagman to film editor. Few if any movie directors have had a more broad-based apprenticeship, laying the foundation for the sheer professionalism that marked his work long before his Oscar-winning triumphs of the mid-1930s. He worked with the best mentors around, including Hal Roach of the *Our Gang* shorts and pie-in-the-face genius Mack Sennett.

The sad-faced and immensely popular Harry Langdon then hired Capra to direct him in three feature movies, *The Strong Man* (1926), *Tramp Tramp Tramp* (1926), and *Long Pants* (1927). The great success of these three movies swelled Langdon's head, and he decided to dispense with Capra and direct himself. It was a fatal mistake—his career went steadily downhill after Capra's departure.

The five major studios in Hollywood in the late 1920s were MGM, Paramount, Warner Bros., Fox, and RKO. There was also another company, the struggling Columbia Pictures, but it was newly headed by the wily, mean, and brilliant, Harry Cohn. Although Capra's next movie, *For the Love o' Mike* (1927), starring Claudette Colbert, was unsuccessful, Harry Cohn named him to the Columbia board of directors in 1928 and gave him carte blanche to produce, write, and direct his own films.

Q. How many movies did Frank Capra direct at Columbia Pictures during his first year at the studio?

   a. five
   b. seven
   c. nine

A. Putting all his experience to use, and learning even more as he went, Capra directed nine movies in his first twelve months at Columbia.

Over the next few years Capra turned out popular movies in a wide variety of genres. There were action movies like *Submarine* (1928) and *Dirigible* (1931); Barbara Stanwyck vehicles, including Capra's first "talkie," *Ladies of Leisure* (1930); snappy comedies such as the silent *That Certain Thing* (1928) and the Jean Harlow hit of 1931, *Platinum Blonde*; and the atmospheric 1932 Stanwyck film *The Bitter Tea of General Yen*, which prefigured the exoticism of *Lost Horizon* five years later.

But in the midst of this diversity, a particular kind of approach to social comedy was taking place. Seen in *Platinum Blonde*, the first of his many movies scripted by Robert Riskin, in *American Madness* (1932), and in *Lady for a Day* (1933), the subject of an idealist facing down corruption was becoming established as the dominant Capra theme.

Q. 1934's *It Happened One Night* was a huge commercial success and became the first movie to sweep the Academy Awards, garnering Best Picture, Best Director Oscar for Capra, Best Adapted Writing for Riskin, as well as Oscars for its stars, Claudette Colbert and Clark Gable. Had Colbert and Gable realized that the movie would prove the highpoint of their careers?

A. No, neither one of them liked the script and both tried to get out of doing it. Capra was happy with the picture, but astonished at its Oscar sweep.

With the enormous success of *It Happened One Night*, Capra moved into high gear. *Mr. Deeds Goes to Town* (1936), *Lost Horizon* (1937), *You Can't Take It with You* (1938), *Mr. Smith Goes to Washington* (1939), and *Meet John Doe* (1941) were all popular successes and brought Capra more Oscar nominations. He won his second directorial Oscar for *Mr. Deeds Goes to Town*, and the picture was also nominated for Best Picture, Best Actor (Gary Cooper), Best Screenplay (Robert Riskin) and Best Sound Recording. *Lost Horizon* was nominated for Best Picture, Best Supporting Actor (H. B. Warner) and won a Best Art Direction award for Stephen Goosson's massive and exotic sets. *You Can't Take It with You* won Capra both the Best Picture and Best Director Oscars, and nominations went to Spring Byington for Best Supporting Actress, Robert Riskin for his script, and it also picked up nominations in the cinematography, sound recording and film editing categories.

In 1939, Hollywood's year of years, against such competition as *Gone With the Wind, Wuthering Heights, Goodbye Mr. Chips, The Wizard of Oz, Stagecoach, Ninotchka,* and *Dark Victory,* Capra still managed to get a Best Director nomination for *Mr. Smith Goes to Washington;* James Stewart was nominated for Best Actor, Claude Rains for Best Supporting Actor, and there were nominations in five more categories as well. The weakest of Capra's films of this period, 1941's *Meet John Doe,* was nominated only for its script, but Gary Cooper's performance in it undoubtedly helped him to corner the Best Actor Oscar for that same year's *Sergeant York.*

Despite all the nominations and awards, and Capra's high standing in Hollywood, some of the more highbrow critics began to complain about the sentimentality of Capra's movies, writing disdainfully about "Capra-corn." The public paid no attention. But there would be no more Frank Capra comedies for a while. With America in the war by the end of 1941, the director joined the Army. Under the overall title of *Why We Fight* Capra produced and sometimes directed a series of distinguished documentaries for the Army, one of which, *Prelude to War,* won him a 1942 Oscar in the documentary category established the previous year.

Capra had in fact made another feature film before joining the Army, an adaptation of the Broadway hit *Arsenic and Old Lace.* The movie was a Warner Bros. production, and the studio held it back, thinking that the rather macabre subject matter about sweet old ladies dispatching lonely widowers for their own good might seem less than hilarious in wartime. But by 1944, with the war dragging on far longer than anyone had expected, they released it to keep Capra's name before the public.

After the war, Capra went back to Hollywood to make what has become his most beloved movie, *It's a Wonderful Life,* starring returned bomber pilot, James Stewart, Capra's favorite actor.

Q. Of the following Capra movies, which was originally the *least* successful at the box office?

    a. *Mr. Smith Goes to Washington*
    b. *Lost Horizon*
    c. *It's a Wonderful Life*

A. The answer is c. Too much had changed in the course of the war, and this quintessential Capra movie seemed old-fashioned to a nation entering a new postwar technological era.

But *It's a Wonderful Life* remained Capra's personal favorite, and its late-thirties' sensibility no longer seems jarring to the untold millions who watch it every Christmas. Dated in 1946, it now seems timeless. But in 1946, it lost over a half-million dollars at the box office.

In fact, none of Capra's great popular hits of the late thirties did much more than break even. People flocked to them, but they were the most expensive movies Columbia Pictures was making. Harry Cohn liked to keep the budget for a movie under six hundred thousand dollars, but several of Capra's movies cost a million and a half dollars, and *Lost Horizon* hit two million. Cohn was willing to let Capra have what he wanted, because it brought the studio respect, prestige, and Oscars.

Hollywood did give both Capra and James Stewart welcome-back Academy Award nominations for *It's a Wonderful Life.*

Stewart drastically changed his image the next year in the hard-bitten *Call Northside 777* and Alfred Hitchcock's *Rope*, but Capra went on making the kind of movie he always had, succeeding on his old level with the 1948 Spencer Tracy/Katharine Hepburn vehicle *State of the Union*, but having much less success with *Riding High* (1950) and *Here Comes the Groom* (1951), two tame Bing Crosby movies.

Capra did not direct again until 1959's *A Hole in the Head*, starring Frank Sinatra. In 1961 he did a remake of his own Oscar-nominated 1933 film *Lady for a Day*, titled *A Pocketful of Miracles* and starring Bette Davis. After that he decided not to direct any more movies, but he wrote a splendid best-selling autobiography, *Frank Capra: The Name Above the Title*. He had indeed been the first director to get his name above the title on a studio picture, even before Cecil B. DeMille or Alfred Hitchcock.

Frank Capra, the little boy from Palermo, remained a beloved and immensely respected member of the Hollywood community for the rest of his life. During his last few decades, one or another of his great movies was playing on television, somewhere in the world, almost every day. What's more, the immigrant from Sicily had succeeded in making the most completely "American" movies of all time. No artist born in another country ever understood his adopted one better. And when he died in early fall 1991, his son could truly say of him, "He really did have a wonderful life."

Bibliography

Adler, Bill. *Baseball Wit*. New York: Crown Publishers, 1986.

Allen, Maury. *Where Have You Gone, Joe Di Maggio?* New York: Dutton, 1975.

Amfitheatrof, Erik. *The Children of Columbus*. Boston: Little Brown, 1973.

Ball, Adrian. *My Greatest Race*. New York: Dutton, 1974.

Blackwell, Earl, ed. *Celebrity Register*. New York: Simon & Schuster, 1973.

Brockway, Wallace, and Herbert Weinstock. *The World of Opera*. New York: Pantheon Books, 1962.

Caso, Adolph. *They, Too, Made America Great: Lives of the Italian Americans*. Boston: Branden Press, 1978.

Davis, Mac. *The Giant Book of Sports*. New York: Grosset & Dunlap, 1967.

Elliott, Lawrence. *Little Flower*. New York: William Morrow and Company, 1983.

Emanuel, Muriel, ed. *Contemporary Architects*. New York: St. Martin's Press, 1980.

Ferraro, Geraldine A., with Linda Bird. *Ferraro, My Story*. New York: Bantam Books, 1985.

Fields, Howard. *High Crimes and Misdemeanors*. New York: W. W. Norton & Company, 1978.

Johnson, Otto, ed. *The 1992 Information Please Almanac*. Boston: Houghton Mifflin, 1992.

Katz, Ephraim. *The Film Encyclopedia*. New York: The Putnam Publishing Group, 1979.

Katz, Lee Michael. *My Name Is Geraldine Ferraro*. New York: New American Library, 1984.

Latil, Pierre de. *Enrico Fermi: The Man and His Theories*. New York: Erikson, 1966.

Malone, John Williams. *An Album of the American Cowboy*. New York: Franklin Watts, 1971.

Marinacci, Barbara. *They Came from Italy: The Stories of Famous Italian Americans*. New York: Dodd Mead, 1967.

Martin, Mick, and Marsha Porter. *Video Movie Guide 1991*. New York: Ballantine Books, 1990.

Monaco, James. *The Encyclopedia of Film*. New York: Perigee Books, 1991.

Murphy, Jim. *The Indy 500*. New York: Clarion Books, 1983.

Null, Gary, and Carl Stone. *The Italian Americans*. New York: Stackpole, 1956.

Rockwell, John. *Sinatra: An American Classic*. New York: Rolling Stone Press/Random House, 1984.

Siegel, Scott, and Barbara Siegel. *The Encyclopedia of Hollywood*. New York: Facts On File, 1990.

Siringo, Charles A. *A Texas Cowboy, or, Fifteen Years on the Hurricane Deck of a Spanish Pony*. Lincoln: University of Nebraska Press, 1966.

Suskin, Steven. *Opening Night on Broadway*. New York: Schirmer Books, 1990.

Thorn, John, ed. *The Armchair Book of Baseball*. New York: Scribners, 1987.

Tomkins, Calvin. *Merchants and Masterpieces: The Story of the Metropolitan Museum of Art*. New York: Dutton, 1970.

Walter, Claire. *The Book of Winners*. New York: Facts On File, 1978.

Wiley, Mason, and Damien Bona. *Inside Oscar*. New York: Ballantine, 1987.

Wyden, Peter. *The Unknown Iacocca*. New York: William Morrow and Company, 1987.